EXPLORING
THE WORLD OF
CHEMISTRY

From Ancient Metals to High-Speed Computers

JOHN HUDSON TINER

EXPLORING
THE WORLD OF CHEMISTRY

First printing, September 2001
Second printing, January 2003

For information write: Master Books,
P.O. Box 727, Green Forest, AR 72638

ISBN: 0-89051-295-7 Library of Congress: 00-102649

Interior Design by Bryan Miller

Printed in the United States of America.

Dedication

This book is dedicated to Samuel Conner Stephens

Illustrations/Photo Credits

All illustrations by **Bryan Miller** unless otherwise noted.
James W. Young 5
The Beinecke Rare Book and Manuscript Library: 23
NASA: 30
Mary Evans Picture Library: 38
The Complete Encyclopedia of Illustration: 56, 97
National Library of Medicine: 88
Image Club, Object Year, CD: 101

Table of Contents

Ancient Metals

Metals such as iron, lead, and tin were important to ancient people. They made tools, spears, shields, dinnerware, and even mirrors from metals. Iron is one of the metals used for centuries. Some ancient civilizations had tools made of iron although they did not have the skill to extract iron from its ore. Where did they get the iron?

One clue to the answer came when Europeans settled in the New World. They discovered that a few tribes of Aztec Indians of South America had tools and knives made of iron. The Aztecs, like the ancient civilizations, did not know how to smelt iron. Where did the iron come from? The Aztecs explained that rocks

ACTION

1. Ancient people had iron tools.

2. Iron resisted efforts to remove it from its ore.

3. The Scott expedition to the South Pole perished in a blizzard when their fuel cans were found empty.

Can You Predict the Reactions?

containing pure iron fell from the sky. They prized the metal more than gold.

The French Academy, a powerful and respected group of scientists, completely discounted the report of falling rocks. Antoine Lavoisier, a famous French scientist, insisted, "The fall of stones from the sky is physically impossible."

Once, an old French clergyman came to the Paris Museum with a stone that he described as having fallen from the sky.

"No," the museum curator said. "You must be mistaken. You should know better. Rocks can't fall from the sky because there are none up there to fall."

The clergyman asked the academy to investigate anyway. A committee of several respected chemists and geologists studied the rocks. They replied, "We regret that in our enlightened age there still are people so superstitious as to believe stones fall from the sky. This peculiar-looking stone is nothing more than soil which has been struck by lightning."

In 1790, the French Academy of Sciences even passed a resolution about the subject. They would no longer investigate reports of objects falling from the sky.

Many museum directors read the academy's report. Did they have any of the stones? People claimed to have seen objects streak through the sky like a flash of lightning. Sometimes the object fell to earth

Leonid Fire Ball

with an ear-shattering bang. They donated the stones to the museums. Museum directors searched through their geology displays for the blackened stones. They found the rocks and hid them from sight.

In 1807 the American chemist Benjamin Stilliman saw such an object fall. He reported to the president of the United States, Thomas Jefferson. The professor invited President Jefferson to come to the field and see for himself the stone that had buried itself upon impact. President Jefferson was an amateur scientist

Ancient weapons

How Egyptians Made Iron

The Egyptians became desperate for iron. One of the rulers of Egypt offered the Hittites an exchange of gold for iron. The Hittites refused, so the Egyptians had to learn to smelt iron themselves.

Coaching iron from its ore is not easy because it is so tightly bound. The Egyptian metal workers believed the ore would release the iron in a hot furnace, the hotter the better. First, they baked wood in closed ovens. Charcoal was formed when wood was heated without oxygen. Charcoal was rich in carbon and burned even hotter than wood. Next, they made a small blast furnace by tipping hollow reeds with clay. They blew through the reeds, sending oxygen through a charcoal and iron ore mixture.

The Egyptian blast furnace worked. They got iron from iron ore.

Chemists know now that charcoal does more than merely generate heat. It takes part in the chemical reaction that releases iron from its ore. Iron ore contains iron combined with oxygen. During smelting, carbon from charcoal frees iron from oxygen's grip by combining with the oxygen.

Iron produced in this way is cast iron. It has impurities, including carbon from the charcoal. Cast iron is hard, but brittle. A sudden blow can shatter it.

The Egyptians learned to remove the impurities by heating cast iron with more iron ore and limestone. The result was wrought iron, a pure form of the metal. It is soft and easily hammered into shape, but is much too soft for most purposes.

Modern steel mill

and a very knowledgeable individual. He declined the invitation. "I find it easier to believe that a Yankee professor would lie than that stones would fall from heaven."

Benjamin Stilliman investigated further. He discovered many honest and dependable people who backed him up. The people claimed they had found rocks that were still hot enough to blister their fingers. Finally, Benjamin Stilliman wrote a book describing the fiery objects. Most American scientists did not believe him.

Rocks did fall from the sky. They still do! The objects come from space and are called meteorites by today's scientists. We call them shooting stars.

Meteorites are from outer space. Most burn up in the earth's atmosphere.

A few survive their fiery trip and plunge to earth. A shooting star is the glowing track in the sky left as a meteor streaks into the earth's atmosphere. Some meteorites are made of rocks, but many are made almost entirely of iron.

Ancient people found these iron meteorites and hammered the pure iron into useful tools. Long before metal workers learned to extract iron from its ores, they found meteorites made of almost pure iron. The image of Diana at Ephesus that "fell down from heaven" in Acts 19:35 may possibly be an iron meteorite.

The Hittites are believed to have been the first to discover the secret of extracting iron from its ore. Until late in the 1800s, the Bible was the only record of the Hittites (Joshua 1:4, for example.) They, along with the Philistines, held the Promised Land of Canaan against the Israelites. For a time, the Philistines captured the ark of the covenant (1 Samuel 4:10–17).

The Hittites built a great empire in Asia Minor. Iron is harder than bronze. Other nations outfitted their armies with bronze knives, swords, and shields. They could not stand against iron weapons. Somewhere between brittle cast iron and soft wrought iron is the most useful and strongest form of iron — steel. The iron of the Egyptians contained just enough carbon to make it a good grade of steel.

Egyptian metallurgists improved upon it even more by quenching it. They heated the iron until red-hot and then suddenly thrust it in cold water. Steel treated in this way is even stronger and harder than regular steel.

Cast iron, steel, and wrought iron differ only in the amount of carbon they contain. Today, structural steel is the most common use of iron. When steel is used as reinforcing rods in concrete, the combination is both rigid and strong.

Iron is cheap and strong, but combines readily with oxygen. The chemical combination of oxygen with a metal or other element is oxidation. Burning is rapid oxidation. Iron itself will burn under certain conditions. For instance, holding a lighted match to fine steel wool causes the steel to burst into flames. Independence Day sparklers have fine iron particles coated on a metal holder. The tiny iron particles sparkle as they burn.

Sparklers have fine iron particles coated on metal holders that sparkle when they burn.

Steel wool and sparklers burn readily. The iron in them is spun very fine. It presents a huge surface area to the air, encouraging rapid oxidation.

The design of the human body takes advantage of iron's ability to react with oxygen. Iron is one of the essential elements in human beings, especially in blood. Hemoglobin carries oxygen from the lungs throughout the body. The iron atoms in hemoglobin readily accept oxygen atoms from the lungs, and release the oxygen to the cells of body tissues. It is oxygen-bearing hemoglobin that gives blood its red color.

Although commonly knows as a "tin" can, this popular food container is actually a thin layer of tin plated over steel.

Larger pieces of iron do not burst into flames, but they react to oxygen nonetheless. Rust is a form of slow oxidation. Although many other metals rust, the oxide coating often protects the metal underneath. This is not the case with iron rust. It flakes away to expose a new layer to the air. Rust continues to do its damage.

Painting prevents rust, or iron can be coated with another metal such as tin to protect it. An Englishman, Peter Durand, patented the tin can in 1810. Tin is nontoxic and does not discolor food. A thin layer of tin is plated over steel. A tin can is a steel can coated with a layer of tin only 1/250 of an inch thick. A tin can is mostly steel, not tin.

Tin is another of the seven ancient metals. During early Bible times people used tin in alloys with copper and lead. Bronze is an alloy of copper with tin. Another important alloy is pewter, a bright and shiny combination of tin with lead. People once used pewter to make cheap kitchen utensils and tableware as a look-alike substitute for expensive silver dishes.

The common name for ordinary metallic tin is white tin. As pure tin gets cold, it undergoes a dramatic change in its physical properties. It turns gray in color. Gray tin is brittle.

British explorer Robert F. Scott led a tragic expedition in 1912 in an effort to be the first to reach the South Pole.

Once, in Russia, tin buttons vanished from soldiers' uniforms. When the quartermaster opened boxes of spare buttons, he found nothing but gray powder. During the long Siberian winter, bitterly cold weather had changed white tin to gray tin.

One of the great tragedies of Antarctic exploration came about because of tin used to solder the seams of kerosene cans. Captain Robert Scott, a British explorer, organized an expedition to try to be the first to reach the South Pole. He led his party across 1,800 miles of ice and snow. At regular intervals, they stored fuel and food for their return. They reached the South Pole on January 18, 1912. Standing on the spot was a marker left there one month earlier by Roald Amundsen, a Norwegian explorer.

Disheartened, the men began their return journey into the face of a blizzard. When the weary men arrived at food and fuel, the tin had turned to powder. The kerosene leaked through the seams. The desperate men raced to the next cache. The cans there were empty, too. The entire Scott party perished in the frozen wilderness, partly because of the little-known fact that tin becomes brittle at cold temperatures.

Tin can be beaten into thin sheets and used as tin foil to wrap foods, especially chocolate candy. However, aluminum will do as well, and the cheaper aluminum has replaced tin. Some people still use the term "tin foil" when actually they mean aluminum foil.

For some reason, people think of tin as a cheap metal, although it is not cheap. They called the first automobiles tin lizzies. People say that cheap radios with poor quality speakers have a tinny sound.

People often use the ancient metals as figures of speech. For instance, a king may rule with a fist of iron. A determined person may be described as having a will of iron. A runner who has become weary is said to have leaden feet. Lead is a heavy metal. When we grow sleepy, we have leaden eyelids because we barely can keep them open. Lead is easily worked into sheets, and rolled into pipes. People of ancient times used lead for water pipes. The Roman name for lead is *plumbum*, the word from which plumber gets its name.

Lead, tin, and iron are three of the seven ancient metals. They are known as the working metals because of their everyday uses.

Ancient lead pipe

REACTION

1. Some meteorites that fell to earth contained pure iron.

2. In a blast furnace, carbon in charcoal combined with oxygen in iron ore to free the pure metal.

3. In the extremely cold weather, cans sealed with tin leaked their precious heating fuel.

> *Answer T or F for true or false; select A, B, C, or D; or fill in the blank for the phrase that best completes the sentence.*

     1. Ancient people hammered the soft, pure iron from _____ into useful tools.

A–D 2. Charcoal is (A. a meteorite that fell from the heavens; B. a type of coal found in the earth; C. made of almost pure oxygen; D. wood that has been heated without oxygen).

T F 3. The only purpose of carbon in smelting iron from its ore is so it will burn and supply heat.

A–D 4. Which of these forms of iron is the purest? (A. cast iron; B. charcoal; C. steel; D. wrought iron).

A–B 5. Cast iron is (A. brittle and will shatter if struck; B. soft and easily hammered into shape).

A–D 6. Steel is quenched by (A. burying it in the earth; B. heating it in an oven for several days; C. heating it white hot and thrusting it into cold water; D. raising it overhead for lightning to strike).

     7. Cast iron, steel, and wrought iron differ only in the amount of _____ they contain.

A–B 8. Rusting is a (A. slow; B. rapid) oxidation.

A–B 9. A tin can is made mostly of (A. tin; B. steel).

A–D 10. The one that looks more like silver is (A. brass; B. bronze; C. gold; D. pewter).

T F 11. Metals maintain their properties regardless of temperature.

A–B 12. The more expensive metal is (A. aluminum; B. tin).

The Money Metals

Gold, silver, and copper are known as the coinage metals because they are often used as money. When Abraham left Egypt after going there following a famine, he described the land as being rich in "cattle, in silver, and in gold" (Genesis 13:2).

Gold, because of its beautiful yellow color and luster, was the most prized ancient metal. It is certainly the first metal mentioned in the Old Testament. Genesis 2:11–12 describes the land of Havilah as having gold, and "the gold of that land is good." Gold is also the first metal mentioned in the New Testament. One of the gifts of the Magi for baby Jesus was gold (Matthew 2:11).

Unlike other metals, gold does not tarnish or rust. Its beautiful luster is unblemished by oxygen and sulfur in the air and it resists most acids. Objects made from gold or covered with it last

ACTION

1. Gold was the most prized of ancient metals.

2. Gold was too soft for many purposes.

3. People who breathed mercury fumes became confused.

Can You Predict the Reactions?

for centuries without tarnishing.

Gold is the most malleable of all metals. Metal workers can flatten it into sheets only a few millionths of an inch thick. Even today, gold foil finds use as lettering on doors of offices, for edges of Bibles, and as inlay on religious paintings. Such gold foil is attractive and does not tarnish or fade with time. It is not very expensive. A little bit of gold goes a long way in making gold foil. A disk of gold no bigger than a dime can be flattened into a thin sheet the size of a bedspread.

Ancient coins

Gold ring

Pure gold is too soft for jewelry and coins. It wears away easily. Goldsmiths mix in copper to make it harder and longer-lasting. They express the purity of gold in carats. Completely pure gold is 24 carats. A 14-carat gold ring has 14 parts of gold by weight with 10 parts of copper by weight.

Like gold, silver is used for jewelry and money. The Old Testament tells how Joseph's brothers sold him to the Ishmaelites for 20 pieces of silver (Genesis 37:28). Later, Joseph became governor of all Egypt. He concealed a silver cup, probably made in Egypt, in the grain sack belonging to his brother Benjamin (Genesis 44:4–12).

In ancient times, metal workers made utensils such as trays, cups, and cutlery of silver. They

also used it as a coinage metal. Like gold, silver is too soft in the pure form. Instead, silversmiths mix copper with it, making it resist the wear of daily use. Sterling silver is an alloy of 11/12 silver and 1/12 some other metal, usually copper.

The last of the coinage metals is copper. The word copper is from *Kupros*, the ancient name for the island of Cyprus, which was famous for its copper mines.

Copper has a reddish-brown color. In pure form, it and gold are the only two colored metals. All other metals are silver-white in color. (Freshly exposed pure iron has a silver-colored surface. However, when exposed to oxygen in the air it rusts quickly to a reddish-brown.)

Silverware

Although ancient people used copper for coins, they used it for other purposes, too. Pure copper is too soft for good knife blades or other cutting tools. It dulls too easily. Instead, metal workers made bronze by melting copper and tin and mixing them together. Bronze is a strong, hard alloy. Another important alloy is brass, made by mixing zinc with copper. Brass takes a better polish than bronze and is even harder.

The Egyptians cut and dressed the stones of the pyramids with tools of copper alloy. Microscopic study of the stones reveals tiny copper particles left behind by bronze hammers and chisels.

Ancient people also used copper alloy such as brass for musical instruments. Paul spoke about the "sounding brass" in 1 Corinthians 13:1.

Copper, like the other coinage metals, is malleable. It can be hammered into shape. In addition, metal workers learned to melt copper and cast it into whatever shape they desired. Many statues were made of copper or bronze.

One of largest bronze statues was the Colossus of Rhodes. This gigantic statue was located on a small Greek island in the Aegean Sea. Its height of one hundred feet earned it a place as one of the seven wonders of the ancient world. Eventually

The Statue of Liberty

the statue fell and was destroyed. It no longer exists.

Great statues are still made of copper. The Statue of Liberty, in New York Harbor, has a copper skin. Copper slowly turns green as it combines with sulfur compounds in the air. This green tarnish forms a protective coating that shields the copper below the surface from any further chemical reaction. Miss Liberty has turned blue-green.

Today copper is largely used for electric wires. Pure copper must be used because the slightest impurity will hinder the flow of electricity. Two of the impurities usually found in copper are silver and gold. The cost of refining copper is offset by the recovery of these valuable impurities.

The Bible mentions six of the ancient metals in a single verse — Numbers 31:22. The Israelites, commanded by Moses, defeated the Midianites. The spoils of the war included gold, silver, brass (copper), iron, tin, and lead.

Lead is used as an example in Exodus 15:10 to show how quickly the Egyptians drowned after the Red Sea covered them: "They sank as lead in the mighty waters."

The Egyptians and other ancient people who lived long ago knew of seven metals. Three are the working metals — iron, tin,

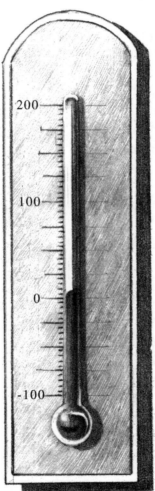

Mercury is used to make accurate thermometers.

and lead. Three are money metals — gold, silver, and copper.

What is metal number seven? It is mercury.

Mercury is a silver-white liquid at room temperature. Metal workers classified it as a metal because of its weight and silvery surface. Mercury looks much like molten silver. A drop of mercury darted about at the slightest movement, as if it were alive. For that reason, people gave the name quicksilver to mercury. Quick is an Old English word meaning "alive."

Mercury, like lead, is a poison. Because it is a liquid, it can be even more dangerous. Even holding a drop of mercury in your hand is not wise. Its vapors are poisonous, too, and should not be breathed. Perhaps you recall the Mad Hatter in the story of *Alice in Wonderland*. At one time mercury was used to treat the felt for men's tall dress hats. People who made these hats often breathed mercury vapor and acted strangely. The mercury fumes damaged their nervous systems. The phrase "mad as a hatter" refers to people who had mercury poisoning.

Mercury is heavier than an equal volume of any other liquid at room temperature. In equal volumes, it is twice as heavy as iron and even heavier than lead. A block of lead floats in a pool of mercury. Mercury forms alloys with most metals except iron. A mercury alloy is an amalgam. Dentists used mercury to fill cavities in teeth. When they mixed gold or silver with mercury, the amalgam was soft and easily molded. Then, it hardened after a few minutes. Because of the way gold or silver held the mercury atoms, there was no health danger from mercury poisoning.

Mercury is the main component of many instruments used in barometers, thermometers, and electric switches.

Like most metals, mercury expands when heated and contracts when cooled. It does so at a uniform rate. Scientists use it to make accurate thermometers. Thermometers for measuring temperature and barometers for measuring air pressure both came into use in the 1600s. Both use mercury. The instruments are reliable guides to how the weather is changing. When the mercury column in a barometer falls, it signals foul weather. When the column of mercury rises, it means the weather should improve.

People of ancient times knew of seven planets. The Roman word planet means "wanderer." They applied the term to heavenly objects that moved about against the background of stars. The seven wanderers are the sun, the moon, Venus, Jupiter, Mars, Saturn, and Mercury.

Stargazers of old times matched the planets and metals together. The sun with its never-failing yellow light matched with gold. The moon, white in the dark sky, matched silver. Venus and Jupiter were matched with copper and tin. Iron, the rusty metal, matched quite nicely the red color of Mars. Saturn, slowly moving and dull, was put with lead.

They identified the liquid silver metal with Mercury, the fastest moving of the planets. Mercury moves rapidly in the sky. The Greeks thought of him as a runner, carrying an important message. He is often pictured with wings on his feet. The Greek name for Mercury was Hermes. The people of Lystra thought Paul was Hermes after he spoke and did a miracle. They tried to worship him, but Paul told them they should worship the living God (Acts 14:12–15).

Learning about the seven ancient metals was a good start to understanding chemistry. What the Egyptians learned was passed on to the Greeks and Romans who found still more uses for the ancient metals.

Unfortunately, chemists became obsessed with the idea of making gold from cheaper metals. Such a discovery would make a person extremely wealthy. Rather than trying to learn more about chemistry, chemists focused on that single idea. They spent all their time trying to make gold from cheaper substances.

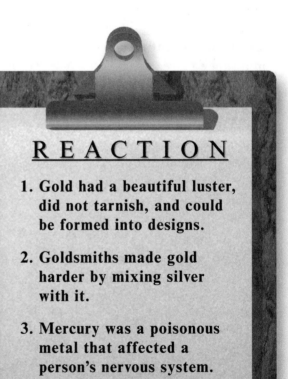

REACTION

1. Gold had a beautiful luster, did not tarnish, and could be formed into designs.

2. Goldsmiths made gold harder by mixing silver with it.

3. Mercury was a poisonous metal that affected a person's nervous system.

1. Gold, silver, and _____ are known as the coinage metals.

A–D 2. The first metal mentioned in both the Old and New Testaments is (A. copper; B. gold; C. iron; D. tin).

T F 3. A 14-carat gold ring is pure gold.

T F 4. Gold resists being beaten into thin layers.

T F 5. Pure silver, unlike gold, is hard enough to resist daily wear.

A–D 6. Bronze and brass are both alloys that contain (A. copper; B. gold; C. iron; D. silver).

A-D 7. Ancient people made musical instruments of (A. copper alloy; B. iron and mercury; C. sulfur and carbon; D. tin and lead).

A–D 8. The Statue of Liberty has a skin of (A. copper; B. gold; C. steel; D. zinc).

9. The seven ancient metals are gold, silver, copper, iron, tin, lead, and _____.

A–D 10. Another name for mercury is (A. calliston; B. cuprum; C. plumbum; D. quicksilver).

T F 11. A block of lead would float in a pool of mercury.

A–D 12. The metal used in thermometers and barometers is (A. barium; B. lithium; C. mercury; D. silver).

13. The seven ancient planets (wanderers) are sun, moon, Venus, Jupiter, Mars, Saturn, and _____.

A-D 14. Ancient people matched the metal gold with (A. Mars; B. the moon; C. Saturn; D. the sun).

A-D 15. The apostle Paul was compared to
A. Mercury, known as Hermes;
B. the moon, known as Luna;
C. the sun, known as Sol;
D. Venus, known as Aphrodite.

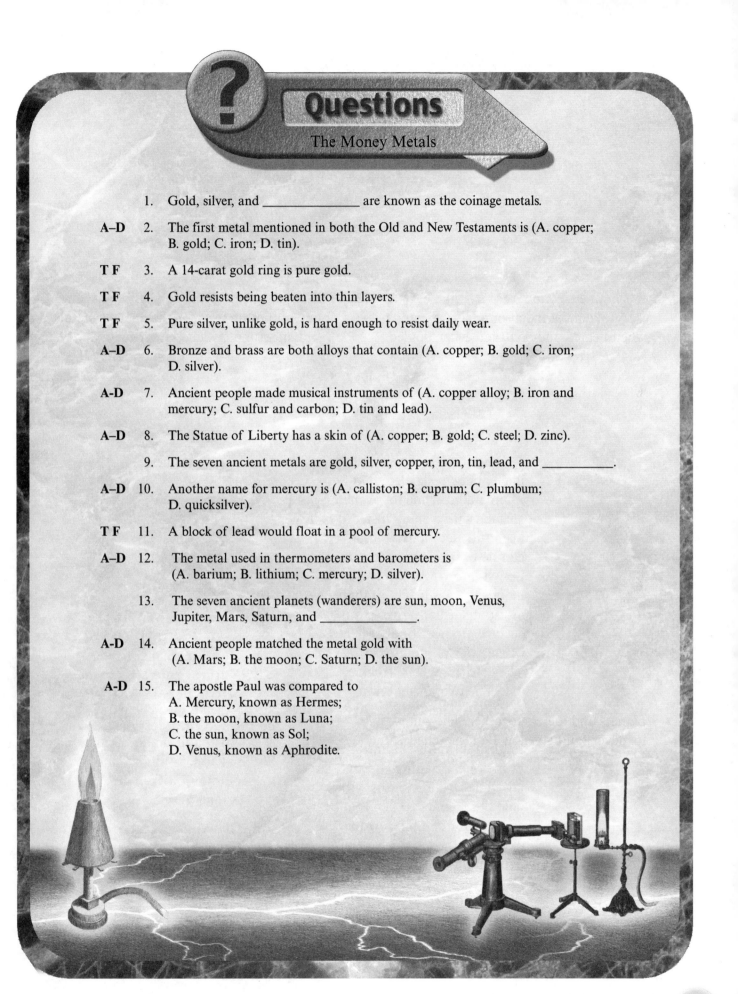

The Search for Gold

Besides the seven metals, ancient chemists also used two nonmetallic elements. A metal has a surface with a shiny luster, it conducts heat and electricity, and it can be beaten into sheets or drawn into wires. Many non-metals are gases. Those that are solids usually have a dull surface, do not conduct heat or electricity, and are brittle. They shatter when struck.

The two ancient non-metallic elements were carbon and sulfur. An old English term for sulphur is brimstone, meaning "burning stone". Sulfur burns with pale blue flames. When set afire, sulfur combines with oxygen in the air to give an irritating, choking gas. The Egyptians burned sulfur in closed buildings to purify the air and drive out pests. When mixed with water the

ACTION

1. Natural rubber became brittle in cold weather and sticky in hot weather.

2. Although made of pure carbon, graphite and diamond differ in properties.

3. Chemists secretly tried to make gold and changed chemistry into alchemy, a false science.

Can You Predict the Reactions?

gas produces sulfuric acid. The King James Version of the Bible mentions sulfur, or brimstone, in Deuteronomy 29:23 and elsewhere. When the heat of a volcano causes sulfur to burn, the result is fire and brimstone.

Matches, fireworks, and black gunpowder all contain either sulfur or sulfur compounds. Gunpowder, the first explosive, is a mixture of sulfur, charcoal, and saltpeter (potassium nitrate). Gunpowder came into use in Europe during the late 1200s. It remained the only known explosive until the 1800s.

Sulfur improves the properties of rubber. Natural rubber is made from latex, a white, milky liquid. Many plants produce latex when their stalks are crushed or cut. The milky juice has a bitter taste. It is poisonous to some animals. Latex seals the injury to the plant and makes it taste bad so animals will not eat it. The most useful latex comes from the bark of rubber trees that grow in the tropics.

In 1823, the Scottish chemist Charles Macintosh patented a raincoat made of rubberized fabric. A raincoat is even today sometimes called a Macintosh. Crude rubber is not perfect in this regard. In cold weather, it became stiff. In hot weather it became soft and sticky. People left raincoats in closets during a hot summer. They opened the closet door to find the raincoats melted together in a terrible mess.

Charles Goodyear, an American inventor, began working on the problem. For ten years, he met with only limited success. Then in 1839 he accidentally dropped a mixture of raw rubber and sulfur on a hot stove. He scraped the mixture from the stove. The rubber pancake stayed flexible when cold and didn't become sticky when warm.

After further improvement, Goodyear patented the process in 1844. He called his invention vulcanized rubber. Vulcan was the mythical Roman god of fire. Vulcanized rubber was tough and waterproof. It sprang back to its original shape even when compressed or stretched.

Goodyear received credit for his discovery. However, it was easily copied and he spent a fortune defending his patent in the process. He received very little money for his many years of labor to perfect the process. He served some time in a debtors' prison and died with a debt of more than half a million dollars.

The single most important compound of sulfur is sulfuric acid. It is the cheapest and commonest of all acids. When a driver turns the key of an automobile, the energy that starts the motor comes from a lead-acid storage battery. The acid in the battery is

Charles Goodyear was the inventor of vulcanized rubber, but died deeply in debt.

sulfuric acid. The battery that starts the car and the vulcanized rubber tires it rides on both depend on sulfur.

Sulfuric acid scrubs oils from the surface of metals. It is used to clean the surface of steel to prepare it for a coating of zinc or tin. The condition of a country's economy can be judged by the amount of sulfuric acid it consumes. The more sulfuric acid a country uses the stronger its economy.

Coal contains sulfur as do natural gas and petroleum. Volcanoes spew out sulfur when they erupt. The sulfur in the atmosphere combines with water and then falls as acid rain. The acid is strong enough to stunt the growth of trees and dissolve limestone used for buildings and monuments.

The other ancient nonmetal is carbon.

Carbon is what burns in wood, charcoal, and coal. The word carbon is from *carbo*, the Roman (Latin) name for charcoal. The New Testament in John 18:18 tells how Peter stood with Roman officers. He warmed himself by a fire of coals while Jesus was being tried. The Romans burned charcoal in shallow metal pans called braziers.

Two other forms of carbon are graphite and diamond. Carbon in graphite forms flat sheets. The sheets easily slide across one another. Graphite is slick. People use it as dry lubricant. It is one of the softest minerals known.

Diamond, on the other hand, is the hardest mineral known. Diamond has its atoms in a pyramid-like structure. Each atom clings to four others, so diamond resists wear. Because of its extreme hardness, diamond finds use as an abrasive for cutting, drilling, and grinding. Oil wells are cut through hard bedrock with

Roman braziers

diamond-tipped drills.

French chemist Antoine Lavoisier lived in the late 1700s in Paris. He believed that diamond was pure carbon. If he were correct, then diamond should burn with an even cleaner flame than the best coal. He collected money from fellow scientists. He bought a diamond to see if it would burn. He placed the gem in a closed container.

With a magnifying glass, Lavoisier focused the rays of sunlight on the diamond. The diamond burned and released carbon dioxide gas.

Antoine Lavoisier went on to make many important discoveries in science. He became France's most renowned chemist. Unfortunately, he was a nobleman and tax collector. During France's Reign of Terror, he lost his head to the guillotine.

Diamond is a form of carbon. Charcoal is also made of carbon. Since the time of Lavoisier, chemists have been fascinated by the prospect of changing charcoal into diamond. The goal was to convert carbon as ordinary charcoal into carbon as highly prized diamond.

French chemist Ferdinand Moissan tried producing synthetic diamond by putting charcoal under extremely high pressure. After an experiment in 1893, he found a tiny fleck of diamond mixed in with the charcoal. It was only one millimeter (1/25th of an inch) long. In triumph, he announced he had made a synthetic diamond.

Other chemists tried to duplicate his process and failed.

Scientists often disagree about the meaning of facts. Two scientists can look at the same data and come to entirely different conclusions. Most scientists shudder at the thought of faking or changing data to strengthen one's argument. For some scientists, the idea of cheating is unthinkable. However, it does happen.

It had happened to Ferdinand Moissan. No one believes Moissan faked his experiment. He was a well-respected scientist who would later win a Nobel Prize

Diamond

for his difficult and dangerous work in producing pure fluorine. Scientists know now that his apparatus was inadequate for the task. He simply could not have produced enough pressure to change coal to diamond. He must have fallen victim to a dishonest assistant. The assistant placed a sliver of diamond in the raw ingredients before the tests began.

Years later, in 1955, a team of scientists did make synthetic diamond. They worked at the laboratories of General Electric. They put carbon atoms under great temperature and pressure, forcing them into the tightly packed pyramid arrangement of diamond. Synthetic diamonds are not fake diamonds. Synthetic ones are as real as the natural ones, except they are made in the laboratory.

The General Electric diamonds were about 0.1 millimeter in size, about the thickness of a human hair. Although larger ones have been made, synthetic

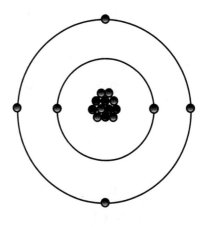

Atomic structure of carbon

Charcoal

Heat

Pressure

Diamond

Making a synthetic diamond

diamonds are too small to be valuable as gemstones. Industry, however, can use synthetic diamonds for diamond-tipped drill bits and other grinding tools.

Changing coal into diamond takes carbon in one form and changes it into carbon in another form. It is a wonderful chemical discovery. The early chemists searched for an even more wonderful process — changing cheap metals into gold.

The idea of changing some cheap metal into gold captured the imagination of ancient chemists. They could think of nothing else. Chemistry, the real science, changed into alchemy, a false science.

Most pencils use a form of lead for a writing substance.

Alchemists based their false science upon the Greek idea of chemical elements. The ancient Greeks believed four simple building blocks made up all nature. They insisted that everything contained some combination of earth, water, air, and fire. If all material was made of only four elements, then they could rearrange the four elements to make gold.

People took the idea seriously. The Roman emperor Diocletian feared that chemistry might successfully produce cheap gold and destroy the economy of the empire. He ordered the destruction of writings on chemistry and banned research into the subject.

Alchemists continued to experiment in secret. Lead was heavy. Sulfur was yellow. Gold was heavy and yellow. Perhaps, they could combine the lead and sulfur to make gold. Alchemists failed repeatedly, but they would not give up. Finally, they concluded they needed a secret ingredient to coach the sulfur into

Alchemists practicing their false science

combining with the lead. They called this missing substance the philosopher's stone. In ancient times, a scientist was known as a natural philosopher.

Alchemists sought money for their fruitless search for the philosopher's stone from rich patrons. They bragged about how their work would benefit their sponsors.

They explained, "Any substance that can change lead to gold must have other wonderful properties as well. The philosopher's stone, once found, will cure disease and restore youth. Its owner will live forever."

The alchemists threw a cloak of secrecy over their work. They guarded their discoveries closely. Reading books written by alchemists were nearly impossible. They used secret symbols and mystical languages. Their writings made sense only to themselves and their trusted assistants. They worked under the motto: "Never reveal clearly to anyone any discovery, but be sufficient unto thyself."

During the Middle Ages from about

A.D. 650 to 1450, chemistry and most other fields of learning came to a standstill in Europe. The Middle Ages are sometimes called the Dark Ages because of the ignorance, fear, and superstition that ruled much of Europe.

Chemistry, after the advances made in Egypt, took a bad turn. Almost a thousand years would pass before chemistry was back on the right course. The person who set chemistry right again was Robert Boyle.

Robert Boyle lived in the 1600s. He was born January 25, 1627. He was 15 years old in 1642, the year Galileo died on January 8, 1642 and Isaac Newton was born December 25, 1642. Robert Boyle became the best known and most respected scientist of his day.

Robert Boyle was born to a family of great wealth. Robert's father, the Great Earl of Cork, was one of the richest and most respected men in the world. His father hired the best tutors for Robert when he was young, and sent him to the best school when he was older.

Robert Boyle studied at Eton in England. He became impatient with many of his classes. Following the lead of the ancient Greeks, science teachers still avoided experiments. Instead, they

Robert Boyle

simply looked for answers in ancient books. Students had to study from approved books. Robert learned geometry from Euclid, astronomy from Ptolemy, medicine from Galen, and logic from Aristotle. These Greek and Roman writers had lived more than a thousand years earlier.

Robert Boyle believed future achievements in science would come by experiments. Robert began meeting each week with a band of like-minded experimental scientists. They held informal talks in each other's homes. Robert called the group of experimental scientists the invisible college because of the many new ideas they dicussed.

Robert urged his fellow scientists to report their experiments quickly and clearly. Even unsuccessful experiments would prove instructive, provided scientists learned from one another's mistakes. Chemists should carefully describe each experiment so others could repeat and study it. "List the compounds and the amounts used," Robert Boyle suggested. "Describe your equipment. Explain how to mix the compounds and in what amounts. State if heat is to be applied and how to separate the products of the chemical reaction."

Robert Boyle continued his efforts to put chemistry on a firm footing. He took the most important step in restoring chemistry as a science. He gave the modern definition of an element. An element, he wrote, could not be made by chemically combining two or more elements. A chemical element was a pure substance that could not be separated into simpler substances by chemical action.

No chemist had ever made gold by mixing together two substances, nor could gold be separated into simpler substances. Countless experiments had failed to alter it in any way. Gold, Robert suggested, must be an element.

Today, chemists know that gold is an element. Gold is made of atoms that are all alike. An atom is the smallest piece of matter and cannot be changed by chemical reactions. Rather than the Greek view of four elements, chemists have identified 90 naturally occurring elements. The count of elements begins with light hydrogen as number 1 and ends with heavy uranium as number 92. The number of naturally occurring elements is 90 rather than 92 because element number 43, technetium, and element number 61, promethium, are not naturally occurring.

Robert Boyle's definition of "element" made the book he wrote, *The Skeptical Chemist*, one of the most important chemistry books ever published. Robert told about his experiments in an easy-to-read style. He didn't try to impress people with difficult language.

A friend of Robert's read one of his books. "You make the study of nature seem so simple," the friend said.

Robert explained, "God would not have made the universe as it is unless He intended for us to understand it."

Robert discovered a new element, phosphorus. It glowed in the dark and burst into flames when rubbed. He put phosphorus to practical use to make the first match. He soaked paper in

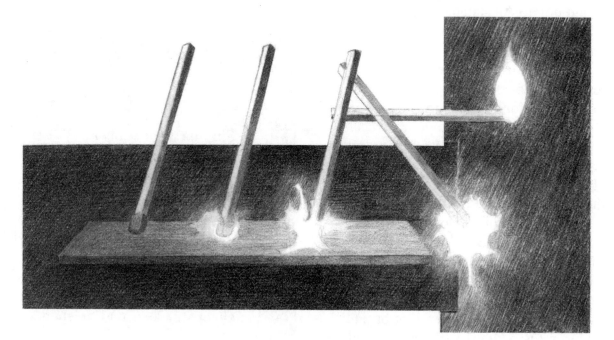

Sulfur-tipped matches are struck against phosphorus-coated paper to create a flame.

phosphorus and dipped a splinter of wood in sulfur. When he drew the splinter of sulfur tipped wood through the paper, the match burst into flames.

Later, he learned that others had discovered phosphorus. They didn't share their discoveries because of a lack of communication. Slow information exchange among scientists hindered the progress of science. How could useful information be spread more quickly?

Robert remembered the invisible college. Such a group could communicate ideas rapidly. Robert and his fellow scientists petitioned Charles II. The king agreed to charter the group of scholars as the Royal Society. Robert and his friends became the first group of scientists to hold regular meetings and exchange scientific discoveries.

The Royal Society still meets today. Its motto is the same as Boyle's: Nothing by mere authority. The motto meant they would not accept statements in the ancient science books as true unless they were proven by experiments.

Robert Boyle achieved worldwide renown as a scientist. He earned a reputation as a person of many talents and as one of the founders of modern science. In 1660 fellow scientists elected him president of the Royal Society. He turned down the office to devote more time to spreading the gospel.

Although Robert Boyle became famous, he remained a humble Christian. The king of England repeatedly offered him high government posts and titles. Robert could have become a nobleman, with a title such as duke, earl, or baron. Robert refused all titles. He never cared for pomp, fame, or public office. He preferred to be known as simply Mr. Robert Boyle, a Christian gentleman.

His interest in religion grew as time passed. Throughout his life he read the Bible each morning. He was a devout Christian and Bible scholar. He learned Latin, Greek, Hebrew, and other related languages to better understand the Word of God. He became a spokesman for Christian causes. Missionaries came to discuss how to spread the gospel. Robert gave great sums of money to hard-working, poor preachers and their families. He provided money for an Irish translation of the Bible and distributed thousands of the Bibles at his own expense.

Robert Boyle died in 1691. In his will, he provided for a series of lectures, not on science, but on the defense of Christianity against unbelievers. The Boyle lectures are still given today.

Today, chemists remember Robert Boyle as the founder of modern chemistry. They consider him one of the ten greatest scientists of all time.

REACTION

1. **Sulphur kept rubber flexible despite changes in temperature.**

2. **Different arrangements of carbon atoms gave hard diamond or slippery graphite.**

3. **Robert Boyle restored chemistry as a true science.**

A–B   1.   Carbon and sulfur are (A. metals; B. non-metals).

A–B   2.   The element known as brimstone is (A. sulfur; B. bismuth).

T F   3.   Sulfur is one of the ingredients in gunpowder.

A–D   4.   Goodyear discovered vulcanized rubber when he (A. added carbon to sulfur; B. heated sulfur with raw rubber; C. put rubber under intense pressure; D. treated rubber with sulfuric acid).

T F   5.   Goodyear made a vast fortune for his invention of vulcanized rubber.

       6.   The single most important compound of sulfur is _____ acid.

A-B   7.   Acid rain is due to (A. carbon; B. sulfur) being spewed into the atmosphere.

       8.   The element that charcoal, coal, graphite, and diamond have in common is _____.

A-B   9.   The one that is slick and can be used as a dry lubricant is (A. graphite; B. diamond).

T F   10.   Synthetic diamonds are fake diamonds and have none of the properties of natural ones.

T F   11.   The primary goal of alchemists was to make gold from cheap metals.

A-B   12.   Science in Europe (A. came to a standstill; B. made great strides) during the Middle Ages.

       13.   The Middle Ages are also known as the _____ Ages.

T F   14.   The schools Robert Boyle attended taught from the latest books by Galileo and Copernicus.

A-D   15.   The invisible college was (A. a gathering of alchemists; B. a gathering of experimental scientists; C. devoted to a study of books by Ptolemy and Aristotle; D. a school for poor students).

A-B   16.   An element (A. can; B. cannot) be separated into simpler substances by chemical means.

A-D   17.   The Royal Society was formed to
A. buy scientific equipment;
B. communicate new ideas rapidly;
C. help write better science textbooks;
D. teach the king about science.

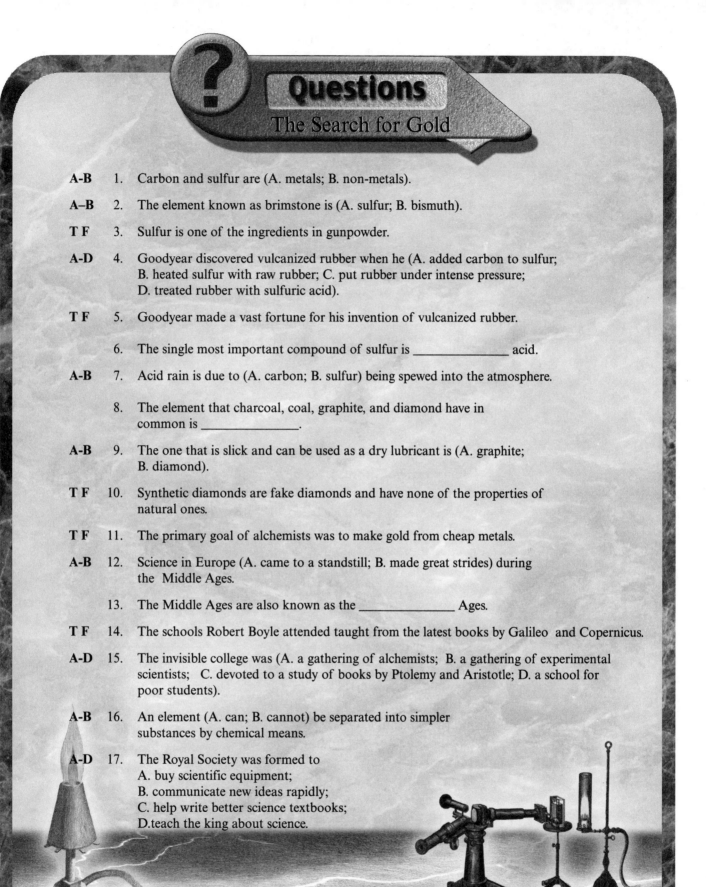

Gases in the Air

Henry Cavendish was one of the most unusual individuals in the history of science. He inherited a large fortune that he devoted to scientific investigations. He never married and lived in a great mansion four miles from London. He could not bear crowds, and would meet only one person at a time. Although he had servants, he instructed them not to show themselves when he was home. They scurried out of his sight as he walked from one room to another. He sent for his meals by leaving a note on the hall table.

Henry Cavendish was born October 10, 1731 in England. He enjoyed experimental science as his only hobby. His skill was in delicate and difficult experiments. He worked under the motto, "Everything is ordered by measure, number, and weights."

ACTION

1. The reaction of the acid with metals gave off a gas that chemists had never seen before.
2. Carbon dioxide that was dissolved in water caused it to fizz.
3. The first explosives contained nitrogen.
4. A brief way of showing chemical elements was needed.

Can You Predict the Reactions?

Henry Cavendish could measure very tiny weights and forces. For instance, Newton's law of gravity states that all objects attract one another. Two balls lying side by side exert a gravitational attraction upon one another. This attraction is so slight that for many years most scientists thought it would be far too weak to measure. Cavendish successfully measured the force of attraction between two lead balls.

In 1776, Cavendish treated several metals with muriatic acid. The reaction of the acid with metals gave off a gas that chemists had never seen before. Cavendish weighed the gas and found it unusually light. Air weighed 14 times as much as an equal volume of the gas. The gas had no color, odor, or taste.

Cavendish's new gas became known as hydrogen. The name hydrogen is from the French word *hydrogéne*, meaning "water generator." This is a good choice for the name because hydrogen combines with oxygen to give water.

Cavendish kept after a problem until he found a solution. Although Cavendish wrote extensive notes, he seldom reported his many discoveries. As soon as he solved one scientific puzzle, he lost interest in it and plunged ahead to the next problem. Henry Cavendish remained an unusual character all of his life. He died alone Febuary 24, 1810 at age 78.

Henry Cavendish

The modern name for muriatic acid is hydrochloric acid. The acid contains one hydrogen atom and one chlorine atom. When it attacks a metal, the chemical reaction combines the metal with chlorine and frees the hydrogen. Reacting a metal with hydrochloric acid is one way to release hydrogen in the laboratory. Another way is to send an electric current through water. The electricity separates the water molecules into oxygen gas and hydrogen gas.

Hydrogen alone does not support combustion. A burning match in a container of pure hydrogen would go out. It also does not support breathing. A person would suffocate in an atmosphere of pure hydrogen, although the gas itself is not poisonous.

Hydrogen with oxygen does burn readily. A stream of hydrogen gas burns in the air with a pale blue flame. If hydrogen is mixed with oxygen or air and then ignited with a spark or flame it explodes violently. Hydrogen makes a good rocket fuel. Liquid hydrogen is lightweight, inexpensive, and burns briskly with liquid oxygen. The exhaust — water — is nonpolluting.

Hydrogen is an abundant element on earth. It is found combined with carbon in petroleum and with oxygen in water. The oceans are a vast storehouse of hydrogen. Hydrogen gas is seldom found in the free state on earth. Although some natural gas wells do release hydrogen, it doesn't stay free long. It either combines with other

Hydrogen makes a good rocket fuel.

elements, or it rises to the upper atmosphere. Rays of sunlight kick hydrogen molecules to such high speeds they escape into space.

Because hydrogen is the lightest element, early chemists used it as a unit to measure the weight of other atoms. By setting hydrogen's weight equal to one, they could use it as a scale to compare the other elements. They expressed atomic weight of an element as the weight of its atom compared to an atom of hydrogen. A carbon atom weighs about 12 times as much as a hydrogen atom. An oxygen atom weighs about 16 times as much. Mercury weighs 200 times as much.

Today, however, chemists use carbon as a standard. They set a carbon atom exactly equal to 12 and measure all other elements against it. With this measuring system, hydrogen has an atomic weight of 1.00797. Oxygen has an atomic weight of 15.9994. Mercury has an atomic weight of 200.59.

In the late 1700s, chemists knew of only three gases: air itself, hydrogen, and carbon dioxide. Today, chemists know that carbon dioxide contains one carbon atom and two oxygen atoms. At that time, chemists didn't know its content. Instead, they called it fixed air. It received this name because it could be fixed in a solid form by reacting it with calcium oxide.

Joseph Priestley was a clergyman and the son of a clergyman. While pastor of Mill Hill Chapel, near Leeds, England, Joseph Priestley became interested in fixed air (carbon dioxide.) He dissolved the gas in water. He described the result as an exceedingly pleasant sparkling water.

Today, carbon dioxide is dissolved under pressure in water used to make soft drinks. When the soda is opened and the pressure is released, the carbon dioxide is released and gives soft drinks their fizz.

Although Scottish chemist Joseph Black had first produced carbon dioxide, Black had not described its properties. To discover a compound in the scientific sense means to learn its properties such as density, color, odor, whether it supports combustion, and how it reacts with other compounds. Priestley's studies of carbon dioxide, which he published promptly, were so thorough he is often given credit for its discovery.

Priestley's interest ranged far beyond chemistry. He wrote several books on many subjects, from church history to Benjamin Franklin's electrical experiments.

In 1774, Priestley received a powerful lens for focusing the sun's rays and generating heat. He thought of all sorts of interesting experiments to do with it. He placed a mercury compound in a closed glass container. With the large magnifying glass, Mr. Priestley focused the sun's rays through the side of the glass test tube. The compound vaporized under the heat. When it cooled, tiny droplets of free mercury clung to the sides of the tube. A gas filled the test tube.

Joseph Priestley

Joseph Priestley tested the gas. A lighted candle flared up and burned brightly. Even a fire almost out came back to life. He thrust an ember into the test tube. The wood burst into flame. Mice placed in a container of the gas became frisky. He breathed some of the gas himself. It seemed to clear his head and make him more awake. He predicted that the new air could have a role in medical science. The pure form of the gas might be helpful for people who have difficulty breathing.

Joseph Priestley had discovered oxygen. Oxygen is a colorless, odorless, tasteless gas. It is an abundant element. More than half of the earth's crust, slightly more than one-fifth of the atmosphere, and two-thirds of the human body are oxygen. A compound of oxygen with another element is an oxide. The mercury compound was mercuric oxide.

Oxygen is a highly active nonmetallic element. Fluorine is the only element more reactive. Oxygen combines with practically any substance. Oxygen is so reactive chemically it would disappear from the atmosphere were it not for plants. Plants, especially trees in large forest areas and algae in the ocean, restore oxygen to the atmosphere.

Any object that will burn in air will burn much hotter and more rapidly in pure oxygen. Suppose a chemist thrusts a glowing splint of wood into a test tube of pure oxygen. The wood promptly bursts into flame. This is one way that chemists test for the presence of oxygen. Rapid oxidation takes place so fast it produces heat and light. Burning wood is an example of rapid oxidation. Most fuels burn because they contain carbon that combines vigorously with oxygen in the air. A spectacular example of rapid oxidation is oxygen gas burning with acetylene gas. Acetylene is a compound of two carbon atoms and two hydrogen atoms. When burned with oxygen, the flame becomes intensely hot, about 6500°C. This is one of the highest temperatures possible by chemical means. An acetylene torch is attached to two containers, one of pure oxygen and the other of pure acetylene. The acetylene flame can cut through thick slabs of steel and other metals. Because oxygen is supplied directly to the acetylene, the torch can burn underwater. Divers use oxygen-acetylene cutting torches to salvage metal from sunken ships.

Slow oxidation releases only small amounts of heat. Rusting is an example of slow oxidation. So is the decay of dead plants and animals. Should the heat of slow oxidation not escape, fire can result. A pile of oily rags may burst into flame of its own accord as heat builds up. Such fires are due to spontaneous combustion.

At age 60 Joseph Priestley had to

leave England because of unpopular political views. He supported the American Revolution against England. An English mob burned his house. He gathered what money he could and fled to the United States with his wife. He'd made friends with Benjamin Franklin years earlier. That great American scientist was dead now, but Thomas Jefferson welcomed Joseph Priestley to the newly independent United States. The last ten years of Mr. Priestley's life were especially pleasant and peaceful ones. Joseph Priestley died in 1804.

Shortly after Priestley discovered oxygen, Daniel Rutherford, a Scottish physician, did an experiment with air. He burned a candle in a closed container until the flame died out. Burning the candle removed oxygen from the air. Mr. Rutherford found that only a part of the air burned. Four-fifths of the original gas in the test tube remained. When he put a burning candle in the container of gas, the flame died immediately. A mouse kept in a closed container of the gas soon died. The gas supported neither life nor combustion.

Daniel Rutherford had discovered nitrogen. Nitrogen is a colorless, tasteless, and odorless nonmetallic gas. Like oxygen, nitrogen is a gas under ordinary conditions. It changes to a liquid if cooled to -195.79°C (-320.42°F), which is very cold.

Priestley's gas (oxygen) encouraged combustion. Rutherford's gas (nitrogen) smothered it. Their actions are the opposite of one another. Nitrogen in the atmosphere helps control combustion. Nitrogen makes open flames possible without leading to disaster. An atmosphere of pure oxygen would present a terrible risk of fire. Only one-fifth of the earth's atmosphere is oxygen. Most of the rest is nitrogen, which partially dampens the burning of oxygen.

Daniel Rutherford

Unlike oxygen, nitrogen is not very active. The bonds holding nitrogen with other elements are easily broken. Nitrogen compounds come apart so quickly an explosion results. One of nitrogen's most important applications is explosives.

The first explosive was gunpowder. It is a mixture of charcoal, sulfur, and potassium nitrate. Potassium nitrate is a compound of potassium, nitrogen, and oxygen. During the 1800s, inventors developed several other explosives, including guncotton, TNT, and dynamite. Each of these explosives has nitrogen as an essential ingredient.

The second important use of nitrogen compounds is in fertilizer. Nitrogen is one of the elements in amino acids, the building blocks of protein. Life requires it. About 3.5% of the human body by weight is nitrogen, mostly in protein.

The earth's atmosphere is 78 percent nitrogen by volume, so theearth has an abundant supply of nitrogen. However, plants cannot take nitrogen gas directly from the air. Instead, they receive their nitrogen from compounds in the soil. Harvesting of crops year after year can exhaust this natural supply of nitrogen.

Crops can fail whenever soils become exhausted of nitrogen. One solution is to plant peas, peanuts, alfalfa, or clover. These plants have nitrogen-fixing bacteria clustered about their roots. The bacteria take nitrogen from the air and combine it with other elements to form solid compounds that the plants can use. Another solution is to put nitrogen back into the soil by spreading fertilizers that contain nitrogen compounds.

For years chemists tried to duplicate the feat of the

Nitrogen-fixing bacteria

simple one-celled bacteria. They tried to develop a process to take nitrogen from the air and make simple nitrogencompounds. Chemists did succeed in combining nitrogen from the air, but it took high temperature and extreme pressure. Chemists still do not understand how nitrogen-fixing bacteria can do the same task at ordinary temperature and pressure.

By the end of the 1700s, the number of elements had grown to well over 25. Practically every chemist had a different way of symbolizing the elements. The special symbols were difficult to draw, difficult to print, and difficult to remember. They differed from one person to the next. Chemists used 20 different symbols for mercury.

In 1814, Jöns Jakob Berzelius, a Swedish chemist, knew there had to be a better way. He made the common sense suggestion to use the first letter from the name of the element as its symbol. Oxygen could be O, nitrogen N, hydrogen H, carbon C, sulfur S, and so on.

Some elements began with the same letter. "Very well," Berzelius said, "add a second letter." For example, carbon's symbol is C, chlorine's symbol is Cl, and cobalt's symbol is Co. Chemists always capitalize the first letter and always leave the second letter lowercase.

The letters as proposed by Berzelius let chemists show chemical reactions easily. Printers could set type for chemistry books using ordinary letters. Chemists quickly adopted Berzelius' system. By international agreements, all chemists everywhere use letters as symbols for chemical elements.

Not all elements have symbols that begin with the first letter of their modern name. Some go under their older Latin (Roman) names. Examples include gold, whose symbol is Au. Silver is Ag,

The Periodic Table of Elements

copper is Cu, lead is Pb, tin is Sn, and mercury is Hg. A few other elements have letters that don't match, such as tungsten whose symbol is W and potassium whose symbol is K.

Chemists can show compounds by chemical symbols, too. They use a small number below the letter to show how many atoms of each element are in the compound. Probably the best-known chemical formula is that of water, H_2O. Water has two hydrogen atoms and one oxygen atom. Carbon dioxide, CO_2, has one carbon atom and two oxygen atoms. Hydrochloric acid is HCl, one hydrogen atom and one chlorine atom. Ammonia is one nitrogen atom and three hydrogen atoms, NH_3.

REACTION

1. Henry Cavendish discovered hydrogen, a gaseous element.

2. Joseph Priestley made the first carbonated beverage with carbon dioxide.

3. Nitrogen compounds separated quickly and exploded.

4. Jöns Jakob Berzelius based chemical symbols on the names of the elements.

A-B   1. Henry Cavendish would be described as (A. shy; B. forward).

A–D   2. Cavendish released the gas hydrogen by exposing metals to (A. ammonia; B. hydrochloric acid; C. carbon dioxide; D. intense heat and pressure).

A-D   3. The name hydrogen means (A. colorless; B. lacking odor; C. lighter than air; D. water generator).

A-B   4. Electricity breaks water molecules into oxygen and (A. hydrogen; B. nitrogen).

A-D   5. If a mixture of hydrogen and oxygen are exposed to a flame (A. a violent explosion results; B. electricity is generated; C. the fire goes out; D. the mixture becomes dry).

T F   6. Hydrogen is an abundant element on earth.

A-D   7. The reason some scientists give Joseph Priestley credit for discovering carbon dioxide is because Priestley (A. had friends who were scientists; B. had political power; C. kept his discoveries secret until the right moment; D. published his thorough studies promptly).

A-D   8. The gas that Priestley released by heating a mercury compound was (A. carbon dioxide; B. hydrogen; C. nitrogen; D. oxygen).

A-C   9. Oxygen makes up about (A. 1/5; B. 3/4; C. all) of the atmosphere.

A-B 10. The chemical activity of oxygen is (A. high; B. low).

A-B 11. The one that supports combustion is (A. nitrogen; B. oxygen).

T F 12. An oxygen-acetylene cutting torch can burn under water.

A-B 13. Rusting of metals is an example of (A. slow; B. fast) oxidation.

A-B 14. The element in the air that prevents fires from burning too quickly is (A. oxygen; B. nitrogen).

15. Give the chemical symbol _____ hydrogen _____ carbon _____ nitrogen _____ oxygen _____ chlorine

16. State the chemical formula _____ water _____ carbon dioxide _____ hydrochloric acid

Electricity to the Rescue

During the early 1800s, chemists continued to search for new elements. They suspected certain compounds contained hidden elements. They believed the compounds contained metals combined with oxygen. They tried to set the metal free from oxygen. Their best efforts failed.

Then, a powerful new tool came to the rescue — electricity.

Scientists knew of static electricity since ancient Greek times. Thales was a Greek scientist who lived about 2,500 years ago. When he rubbed amber with wool, the amber attracted bits of thread and lint by static electricity. The word electricity is from *elektron*, the Greek word for amber.

New facts about electricity didn't change much for two thousand years. Then in the 1500s William Gilbert, an English physician, showed that substances other than amber could be given an electric

ACTION

1. A blast furnace could not set some elements free from their ores.

2. Chemists needed a dependable supply of electricity.

3. Potash and soda ash were thought to contain metallic elements.

Can You Predict the Reactions?

charge. He rubbed glass rods and rock crystals with wool and fur. They became charged, as did rods of hard rubber. You can try his experiment today by rubbing a plastic comb briskly through clean, dry hair. The comb becomes charged. It will attract small pieces of paper.

Objects charged by rubbing have a static electric charge. The word static means "at rest." Sometimes, when you bring an object near a charged body, the static electricity discharges. It makes a crackling sound. A tiny spark jumps from the charged body.

Benjamin Franklin, the American scientist and statesman, wondered about static electricity and lightning. Perhaps the spark of a static charge was merely a miniature lightning strike.

In 1752, Benjamin Franklin flew a kite in a lightning storm. He drew lightning down the kite string and tested it. It had all the properties of static electricity. This

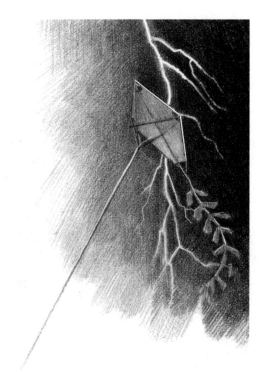

difficult and exceedingly dangerous kite experiment settled the matter. Lightning was a big discharge of static electricity. Thunder from lightning and the crackle of a static discharge are both caused by electricity suddenly heating the air. The rapidly expanding air causes the sound.

Scientists continued to experiment. They made static electricity by friction. One static generator rubbed a ball of sulfur against a felt pad. These clumsy, hand-cranked static generators required constant attention. Often they gave but a single spark of electricity.

By the late 1700s work on static electricity had reached a dead end. What scientists needed was a steady stream of electric current. An electric current is electricity in motion.

In the 1790s, Luigi Galvani, an Italian medical scientist, made an unusual discovery. He knew that static electricity would cause living muscles to twitch. Many scientists had felt the shock of static electricity. The sudden discharge caused their

Benjamin Franklin

muscles to jerk suddenly and without control. While dissecting a dead frog, he touched one of the legs with a scalpel. The leg twitched. He investigated further and found that static electricity caused the legs to twitch.

Galvani knew that Franklin had proven that lightning was a form of static electricity. Would lightning cause the legs to twitch? Galvani attached frogs' legs to brass hooks and hung them against an iron grill outside his laboratory window. Yes, the legs twitched during a thunderstorm. They also twitched at other times, even without lightning. The legs twitched whenever they touched both the brass hook and iron grill.

More experiments uncovered a mystery. Suppose he touched the legs of a dead frog with two different metals, such as copper and zinc. The legs would jerk. Somehow, the combination of frog's legs and two metals generated electricity.

Galvani could not explain his observation, but he reported his results. His report came to the attention of another Italian, Alessandro Volta.

Alessandro Volta was one of nine children. He was a slow learner and did not talk until he was four years old. At first his family worried that he might be disabled. However, after he started to school he caught up with the other children and passed them. He became a successful scientist.

Volta demonstrating battery to Napoleon Bonaparte in 1801

Alessandro Volta read about Galvani's experiments with twitching frogs' legs. What caused the electricity?

Volta did away with the frogs' legs. Instead, he soaked a cloth disk with salt water. He touched two different types of metal to the cloth. A faint electric current flowed. Chemicals alone produced an electric current. In 1800, Volta built a device that would produce a large flow of electricity. He separated small disks of copper and zinc with cardboard soaked in salt water. When he connected a wire to the top and bottom of the stack, he was rewarded with a steady electric current. He generated a stronger current by stacking together several of the individual cells.

A battery is a series of electric cells working together. Alessandro Volta had made the first electric battery. It produced a reliable supply of electric current. No one had to turn a crank. The battery had no visible moving parts.

Today, scientists understand that subatomic electrons move in the wires. The human eye cannot see electrons nor can even the best optical microscope. Yet, tiny electrons are the cause of both current electricity and static electricity. Electrons in motion make current electricity, and electrons at rest make static electricity.

Volta's battery opened a whole new field of study. He received many honors. His fellow scientists named the force that puts electrons in motion after him the "volt."

Luigi Galvani has been honored, too. Chemists learned how to use electricity to coat sheets of iron with zinc to keep the iron from rusting. They call it galvanized iron. Scientists named an instrument designed to measure electric current after him a "galvanometer." The word "Galvani" entered the language as a figure of speech. When a person is galvanized into action, he reacts quickly as if energized by an electric shock.

Englishman Humphry Davy put electricity to use in a new way. He came from a middle-class family and his father appeared to make a good income. Davy enjoyed fishing and exploring the English countryside. However, when his father died, Davy discovered that his father was deeply in debt. Over the next few years, he and his mother succeeded in paying back all the people to whom the family owed money.

Davy had not been doing well in school, so he became an assistant to a druggist. The study of chemicals fascinated him. At the drugstore he began a course of self-education in which he repeated every chemical experiment that he'd read about and many others never before attempted. Unfortunately, Humphry Davy seldom exercised good safety measures with chemicals. Repeatedly his chemical experiments produced explosions. Davy's work at the druggist's shop ended abruptly. The owner of the shop dismissed the boy before he blew up the business.

Humphry Davy gained a position as chief research chemist at a hospital devoted to testing medical uses of new gases. Davy unwisely tasted and sniffed new chemicals. He nearly suffocated himself while experi-

Humphry Davy

menting with a potent mixture of hydrogen and carbon monoxide. At age 20, Davy became superintendent of the hospital. Later, he became the chief researcher at the Royal Institution of Great Britain in London.

About 1805, Humphry Davy began experimenting with electricity. He built a battery like the one invented by Volta. He attached a wire to each of the two terminals of the battery. He dipped a wire on opposite sides of the container of water. When the current flowed, bubbles of gas bubbled up from around the wires. Hydrogen gas bubbled up on one side. Oxygen gas formed on the other side.

Davy thought if an electric current can separate oxygen from hydrogen, then it could separate other elements from oxygen. Until then, chemists separated metals from their ores by heating them. Sometimes chemists added carbon or another chemical to draw the oxygen off, freeing the metal. Chemists suspected that several substances contained metallic elements. These substances included lime, magnesia, potash, and soda ash. Their usual refining methods of heating the ore with carbon in a blast furnace didn't free the metals. Oxygen clung tightly to the metals. To pry it away took stronger measures.

Davy found the stronger measure in electricity. He built a battery of 250 individual voltaic cells. It was the strongest battery in the world.

He sent a strong current through molten potash. Silvery beads of a new

Davy separating elements using electrical currents

metal formed as droplets on one of the electrodes. He called it potassium. Davy became so excited he jumped around the laboratory in delight. Only a week later he freed a metal from soda ash and called it sodium. Then, in short order he refined four new metals with electrolysis. They were barium, strontium, calcium, and magnesium. No other chemist had discovered so many elements so quickly.

His discoveries of new elements made him famous. In 1812 he was knighted and became Sir Humphry Davy.

His lack of caution around chemicals took their toll. An explosion nearly blinded him. His sniffing and tasting chemicals left him weak. Sometimes he could not get up from his bed. Davy still had a clear mind. He continued to make top-rank discoveries.

During the 1800s, coal fueled the industrial revolution. Each year coal miners who worked in shafts sunk deep in the earth suffered terrible tragedies by explosions in the mines. Miners carried lanterns with open flames. Gas and coal dust

collected in the mines. Every so often, the flame from the lantern would ignite the gas or coal dust. The resulting explosion killed miners and shut down the mines.

Davy invented a safety lamp. The lamp burned oil, but Davy surrounded the open flame with a metal screen. The screen absorbed the heat but allowed oxygen to pass to the flame. Explosive gases outside the lamp would not ignite. The safety lamp dramatically reduced the danger of fires and explosions. For the first time miners were reasonably safe as they dug the coal.

Selling the rights to manufacture the safety lamp would have made a fortune for Davy. Instead, he refused to patent it so mining companies would more quickly adopt its use. He became a hero to miners.

In 1820, Davy became president of the Royal Society. His years of sniffing and tasting chemicals left him weak. He had to spend more time in bed and depended on his assistant Michael Faraday to carry on his work. One of his final inventions was the dazzling bright arc light. A powerful current of electricity jumped across the gap between two carbon electrodes and generated light. It was the first attempt to use electricity to give light. For more than a hundred years, arc lights were used in theaters for spotlights and outside as search lights.

Davy wrote several books on chemistry, including one on how to improve agriculture. His last book was about his early days and his passion for fishing, *Days of Fly Fishing*. Sir Humphry Davy died in 1829 at the age of 50. His lack of caution around chemicals probably cut his life short by at least 25 years.

Two of the elements Davy discovered are potassium and sodium. They are members of a group of six elements known as the sodium family. They are also known as the alkali metals. Alkali is a word meaning "from the ash." Members of the family are lithium (Li), sodium (Na), potassium (K), rubidium (Rb), cesium (Cs) and francium (Fr).

Members of the sodium family are metals. They have a silvery luster. They conduct electricity and heat. They can be drawn out into long wires and hammered into thin sheets. But some of their properties are unusual. They are so soft you can cut them with a knife. They melt at low temperatures and are lightweight. Sodium and potassium are so light they would float in water.

Sodium family metals are extremely active chemically. They are so caustic they will burn your fingers simply by touching them. The burn is due to the metal stripping oxygen from the compounds found in the human body. They react immediately with oxygen in the air. Chemists never find them free in nature. Sodium exposed to air quickly oxidizes (rusts) and crumbles.

The name sodium comes from soda ash. The chemical symbol is Na, from *natrium*, the Latin (Roman) name for one of its compounds.

The pure metal is a used in sodium vapor lamps. The compounds of sodium have far more uses than the pure metal. Chemists use soda ash to make soap and ordinary window glass. Photographers use sodium thiosulfate to prevent their pictures from fading. Baking soda (sodium bicarbonate) is used in cooking and to absorb odors. Of course, the best-known and most abundant compound of sodium is ordinary table salt, NaCl.

Potassium is named for potash. The chemical symbol is K from *kalium*, an old name of one of its compounds.

Potassium is even more chemically reactive than sodium. If a sample of potassium is dropped into water, it strips oxygen atoms from water molecules and frees hydrogen gas. The heat of the reaction causes potassium to melt and burn even faster. The hydrogen gas ignites. In

Table salt (NaCl)

other words, potassium causes water to burn.

When chemists use sodium family metals in the laboratory, they must be careful to avoid starting a fire. Once the reaction begins with a member of the sodium family, the fire is difficult to put out. The first thought is to douse the burning metal with water. But that only adds fuel to the reaction. Instead, laboratory workers keep buckets filled with salt, soda ash, or dry sand on hand. They dump the buckets of sand over the burning metal to smother it.

Lithium, Li, is the lightest member of the sodium family. It is the lightest of the solid elements. Gold, a dense metal, is 36 times as heavy as an equal volume of lithium. Lead is 21 times as heavy. Aluminum, a metal we think of as light in weight, is 5 times as heavy as lithium. Some woods such as oak are heavier than it is. Lithium will float in water.

Alloys of lithium are exceptionally useful because they are so lightweight.

One of its alloys with magnesium has the best strength-to-weight ratio of any building material.

When heated red hot, lithium will combine with hydrogen to form lithium hydride, LiH, a solid. A small amount of lithium can combine with great volumes of hydrogen. During the early days of flying across the Atlantic, pilots carried lithium hydride pellets as portable hydrogen generators. If their planes went down in the ocean, the pilots mixed the pellets with water which released hydrogen. The gas inflated lifeboats and balloons. They used the balloons as signals, or to carry aloft a radio antenna for emergency broadcasts.

Lithium makes a good battery. It generates a lot of electricity for its light weight. Lithium batteries power cameras and calculators. A lithium battery works even in cold weather. It can be left on the shelf for a long time without running down.

Lithium and the other sodium family metals give off distinctive colors when exposed to a flame. Sodium glows a yellow color; potassium is violet. Rubidium emits magenta, a combination of red and violet. Cesium lights up with a beautiful sky-blue color. Chemists can identify lithium by the flame test, too. When heated, it gives off a deep red color known as carmine. Lithium is often used to give fireworks a red color.

One of the interesting stories in chemistry is how the flame test solved an everyday mystery. In 1891, Robert Wood stayed at a boarding school near the university he attended in Baltimore. The students didn't trust the cook. They believed she made their morning meal

Lithium battery

from leftovers collected from their plates after dinner the previous night. How could the boarders prove their suspicions?

One night the cook served a steak for dinner. Robert Wood sprinkled the meat with lithium chloride. It is as harmless as ordinary table salt. It tastes the same, too. Robert Wood left untouched several big slices of meat.

The next morning the students collected a sample of the stew the cook served them for breakfast. They examined the sample with the flame test. The unmistakable deep red color of lithium colored the flame. The thrifty cook had been feeding her guests the scraps of one meal for the next.

REACTION

1. Electricity drew new elements from their ores.

2. Alessandro Volta made the first electric battery.

3. Humphry Davy used electricity to discover potassium and sodium.

42

T F   1. Static electricity was unknown to the ancient Greeks.

A-B   2. Objects charged by rubbing have a (A. current; B. static) electric charge.

A-D   3. Benjamin Franklin's kite-flying experiment proved that lightning (A. can charge a battery; B. can kill a turkey; C. helps clouds discharge rain; D. was a big discharge of static electricity).

A-D   4. The one who discovered that frogs' legs would twitch when touched by two different metals was (A. Alessandro Volta; B. Benjamin Franklin; C. Humphry Davy; D. Luigi Galvani).

A-D   5. Alessandro Volta built the first (A. arc lamp; B. device to make electricity by friction; C. battery to produce electric current; D. miner's safety lantern).

A-D   6. Current electricity is due to the motion of (A. electrons; B. frog legs; C. neutrons; D. protons).

A-D   7. The one who unwisely tasted and sniffed new chemicals was (A. Benjamin Franklin; B. Humphry Davy; C. Michael Faraday; D. Robert Wood).

A-D   8. Davy discovered potassium by treating potash with (A. a hot arc lamp; B. heat from a large burning lens; C. carbon in a blast furnace; D. electricity from a strong battery).

9. An arc light generates light as electricity jumps across the gap between two _____ electrodes.

A-B   10. Members of the sodium family are (A. metals; B. nonmetals).

A-B   11. The members of the sodium family are chemically (A. active; B. inactive).

A-B   12. The one used to put out a sodium fire in the laboratory is (A. water; B. dry sand).

A-B   13. Compared to other metals, lithium is (A. light; B. heavy).

A-D   14. Robert Wood used the flame test to prove that
A. lithium causes water to burn;
B. lithium could be used as table salt;
C. lithium is found in fireworks;
D. the cook used leftovers to make stew.

Search for Order

Ancient people knew of seven metallic elements (gold, silver, copper, iron, tin, lead, and mercury) and two nonmetallic elements (carbon and sulfur). The alchemists during the Middle Ages added five new elements. From the time of Robert Boyle (about 1650) to the time of Henry Cavendish (late 1700s), chemists discovered six more metals and four gases.

Elements are the building blocks that make compounds. Table salt (sodium chloride) is made of the elements sodium and chlorine, NaCl. Sulfuric acid is made of hydrogen, oxygen and sulfur, H_2SO_4. Although the number of elements is small, the number of compounds they form is large.

By the start of the 1800s, chemists had found 25

ACTION

1. The large number of elements and their properties became confusing.

2. Chemists were baffled by a number of annoying problems such as atomic weight.

3. The periodic table of the elements had gaps.

Can You Predict the Reactions?

elements. In the next 30 years, the pulse of chemical discovery quickened. The number of elements doubled to 60. Their properties varied widely. Some were poisonous gases like chlorine. Others were inactive metals like platinum. Chemists couldn't remember all the facts about the many new elements and their compounds.

Scientists who saw the intelligent design in creation believed that simple principles governed nature. Many chemists such as Robert Boyle believed the Creator put this order in nature. Because of a single Author, the universe was consistent and predictable. Time and again scientists discovered that the most confusing observations could be replaced with a few simple laws. In physics in the late 1600s, Isaac Newton summarized a vast amount of information about motion and force with the three laws of motion and the law of gravity.

Chemists knew thousands of facts about the chemical elements. They hoped someone with Newton's ability would summarize the facts into a compact and easily understood form. Unfortunately, all attempts to arrange the elements in a useful pattern failed. More than 150 years after Newton, chemists still had no way to simplify their subject.

In the 1850s, a Russian chemist decided to tackle the problem. Dmitri Ivanovich Mendeleev was the youngest son

Dmitri Mendeleev

in a family of 17 children. His father was the principle of a high school in their hometown of Tobolsk, Siberia, in Russia. Shortly after Dmitri's birth, his father became blind. His mother supported the family by managing a glass factory in a nearby town. Dmitri received a scientific education from a political prisoner. The Russian government had banished the man to Siberia. Dmitri proved to be a bright student and willing to learn.

When Dmitri was 13 years old, his father died. The next year his mother lost her job when the glass factory burned. His mother was aware of her young son's exceptional ability in mathematics and science. She made the heroic decision to leave Tobolsk and travel more than 1,500 miles to Moscow. She planned to enroll him at the University of Moscow. However, residents of Siberia were not considered good academic material. Dmitri was refused admission.

His mother gave up on Moscow but not on her son's education. She traveled another 500 miles to St. Petersburg. The university in that city also closed its door to the Siberian mother and her son. Finally, only weeks before her death, Dmitri received admission to a college that trained teachers.

He not only qualified as a teacher, but finished college at the top of his class and won a gold medal for his scientific studies. He continued to study for an advanced degree in chemistry. In 1857 his ability came to the attention of the university officials at St. Petersburg. They now asked the student they had turned away to join their faculty.

Before beginning at the university he went to Germany for further studies. He was fortunate to attend one of the most successful scientific gatherings ever held. In 1860, chemists from all over the world gathered for the First International Chemical Congress, which met in Karlsruhe, Germany. For almost 50 years chemists had been arguing about the meaning of terms such as atomic weight, formula weight, the nature of gases, and many other topics. At the conference, they came to agreement on a number of annoying problems.

Atoms are very small. Because of their small size, chemists could not count the atoms that took part in chemical reactions. Instead, they weighed the ingredients going into the reaction and weighed the products after the reaction. Their conclusions about the numbers of atoms in the reaction were based on atomic weights. They selected hydrogen as the standard and stated the weights of atoms of other elements in terms of hydrogen. With this agreement, chemists calculated a list of atomic weights for most elements. Hydrogen was the first and lightest element and uranium was last and heaviest on the list.

In 1861, Dmitri was back at St. Petersburg teaching chemistry. He found most of the chemistry textbooks in Russia to be woefully inadequate. To solve the problem he wrote his own textbook. For years, it was considered the best available.

Dmitri was a good teacher who cared about his students. Many of his students became discouraged at the mass of information they had to learn to master chemistry. Chemists had discovered more than 60 elements. The facts about each element had become almost too extensive for anyone to comprehend. Learning about the many different compounds, which numbered in the millions, was even more difficult. Mendeleev believed an organized table of the elements would help his students.

Dmitri Mendeleev began his project in the late 1860s. For each of the 60 elements, Mendeleev wrote out a note card. He described the element as a metal, nonmetal, or gas. He entered the atomic weight and other properties of the element and its compounds. What was the element's color and its melting and boiling temperatures? What was its density? Did the element form acids, bases, or salts? Did it combine with oxygen? What were the chemical formulas for its most important compounds?

He cleared one wall of his laboratory. There he hung the cards. He would study the arrangement and see if any pattern emerged.

Dmitri decided that one important property of an element was its atomic weight. Each element had an atomic weight that differed slightly from the one next to it. The lightest element was hydrogen with an atomic weight of 1.0. The next six lightest elements were lithium, Li; beryllium, Be; boron, B; carbon, C; nitrogen, N; oxygen, O; and fluorine, F.

Element	Li	Be	B	C	N	O	F
Atomic Wt.	6.9	9.0	10.8	12.0	14.0	16.0	19.0

Dmitri believed another important property of an element was its chemical combining power. One atom of hydrogen combined with chlorine to give hydrochlo-

Li	Be	B	C	N	O	F
lithium	beryllium	boron	carbon	nitrogen	oxygen	fluorine
Na	Mg	Al	Si	P	S	Cl
sodium	magnesium	aluminum	silicon	phosphorus	sulfur	chlorine

ric acid, HCl. Chlorine had a combining power of one. Oxygen had a combining power of two because it combined with two hydrogen atoms to give water, H_2O. Nitrogen took three hydrogen atoms to give ammonia, NH_3. Nitrogen had a combining power of three. Carbon required four hydrogen atoms to make methane, CH_4, so its combining power is four.

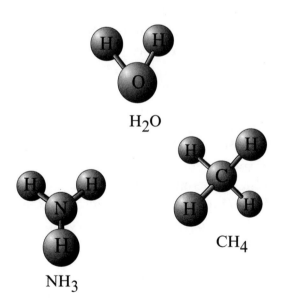

H_2O

NH_3

CH_4

Chemists gave the name "valence" to the number of hydrogen atoms that are needed to combine with an element. Dmitri recorded the valence for the elements from lithium through fluorine.

Element	Li	Be	B	C	N	O	F
Valence	1	2	3	4	3	2	1

Valence rose and fell. It began as one for lithium, rose to four for carbon, and fell again to one for fluorine.

Dmitri began to see a pattern. He organized the elements by atomic weight and chemical combining power (valence).

The next element by atomic weight was sodium, Na. Sodium and lithium were both metals, both had the same valence. Both were chemically very active metals. Because of their similar properties, he put sodium below lithium. The other elements fell in order based on their atomic weight, valence, and chemical properties. He was pleased to see that chlorine fell below fluorine. Those two elements both had a valence of one, both were nonmetals, and both very active chemically. Fluorine and chlorine formed similar compounds.

What about hydrogen? It had a valence of one. Should it go in the column with sodium or in the column with chlorine? Despite having a valence of one, it was a nonmetallic gas, so it did not belong with lithium and sodium. On the other hand, it had none of the chemical properties of fluorine or chlorine. Dmitri decided hydrogen was a special case and hung it at the top in a row by itself.

Mendeleev's Periodic Table In Symbols

H																	*
Li	Be											B	C	N	O	F	*
Na	Mg											Al	Si	P	S	Cl	*
K	Ca	*	Ti	V	Cr	Mn	Fe	Co	Ni	Cu	Zn	*	*	As	Se	Br	*
Rb	Sr	Y	Zr	Nb	Mo	*	Ru	Rh	Pd	Ag	Cd	In	Sn	Sb	Te	I	*
Cs	Ba	La	*	Ta	W	*	Os	Ir	Pt	Au	Hg	Tl	Pb	Bi	*	*	*

Dmitri began the next row. The active metal potassium, K, fell into its proper place below sodium and lithium. On the other side bromine, Br, fell below chlorine and fluorine. Here and there, an element fell in a family to which it did not belong. Mendeleev moved the element over and left a gap.

Why gaps? Dmitri believed they would be filled later as chemists discovered new elements. The complete table looked something like this (*see table above*)**.** The asterisks (*) show the location of missing elements. You will recognize some of the elements by their chemical symbol.

In March 1869, Dmitri Mendeleev revealed his table to the Russian Chemical Society. At first, some chemists objected to the arrangement. They thought he mixed mathematics and chemistry. Dmitri, however, did not apologize. "Any system based on numbers," he said, "is better than other systems that do not have numerical support."

Dmitri silenced the critics by a bold step. For three of the undiscovered elements, he described their properties in careful detail. He predicted the density, melting and boiling temperatures, atomic weight, and how they would combine with oxygen and sulfur.

What element would fill the space below aluminum, Al? Dmitri predicted its atomic weight to be about 68. He set the density at about five times that of water. He predicted it would have a low melting point but a high boiling point. He even predicted how it could combine with oxygen. Two atoms of the missing element would combine with three atoms of oxygen. The formula would be X_2O_3, with X representing the unknown element.

In 1875 a French chemist discovered a new metallic element. It had the second lowest melting temperature of any metal. Only mercury was lower. The new metal would melt on a warm day. Yet, it did not vaporize until heated to nearly 2,000°C (3,632°F). The density and atomic weight were as predicted. No one doubted that the Frenchman had discovered Mendeleev's missing element. The French chemist named the element gallium, Ga. *Gallia* is the Latin name for France. Gallium was placed in the periodic table below aluminum.

As the years passed, chemists found all three of Mendeleev's missing elements. His predictions matched their actual properties closely.

Mendeleev showed that the properties of the elements repeat from one row to the next. This is the periodic law. Periodic means to recur at a regular cycle. Chemists called Mendeleev's table the "Periodic Table of the Elements."

Practically every chemical classroom and laboratory has a version of the periodic chart hanging on the wall. It does not look the same as Dmitri's original chart. New elements were added and it was modified to better fit on a sheet of paper. What Mendeleev discovered was the law that the properties of elements repeat. The periodic table is merely a way to show the periodic law.

The up and down columns show families of related elements. The sodium family is lithium, sodium, potassium, and the three elements under it. A family is usually named by the best-known element in the family. That may not be the first element. For instance, the chlorine family (fluorine, chlorine, bromine, iodine, astatine) is named after chlorine because it is better known than any other member of its family.

Within a single family, most of the chemical properties are very similar. Rather than having

to memorize information about each element the chemist has only to learn about a single element in the family. The other elements in the sodium family form compounds similar to those of sodium. Sodium and chlorine combine to give table salt, NaCl. Lithium also combines with chlorine, LiCl, as does potassium, KCl.

Now it is easy to understand how Dmitri predicted the formula for the combination of oxygen with the missing element, gallium. Right above gallium in the periodic table was aluminum. Chemists knew that aluminum oxide had two aluminum atoms and three oxygen atoms, Al_2O_3. Because the missing element was in the aluminum family, Dmitri gave it a similar formula, X_2O_3.

The periodic chart was a powerful tool for understanding chemistry. His table, first proposed in 1869, became a trustworthy guide to further chemical discovery.

Dmitri Mendeleev became one of the most celebrated chemists in the entire world. Chemists from other countries came to St. Petersburg to study with him. Dmitri gave credit to his mother for his success. In 1887, Dmitri dedicated a book to his mother. He said, "She instructed by example, corrected with love, and to devote her son to science she left Siberia with him, spending her last resources and strength."

Thinking of his mother reminded Dmitri of the hardships the poor peasant

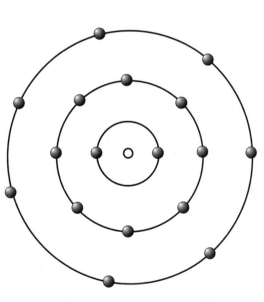
Electronic configuration of chlorine

Mendeleev applied chemistry in a small experimental farm. His methods helped to improve the yield and quality of crops.

farmers in the rural areas of Russia faced as they eked out a living. He started a small experimental farm to apply chemistry to farming. His methods helped improve the yield and quality of the crops. His success helped all Russians.

In 1890 he took the side of students in a protest against the school administration. Angry university officials dismissed Dmitri Mendeleev from his post. The Russian government, however, realized that his skills were too important to remain idle. They appointed him to oversee the bureau of weights and measures.

Chemists honor Dmitri Mendeleev in the periodic table that he discovered. They named element number 101, discovered in 1955 by American nuclear chemists, mendelevium, Md.

REACTION

1. Dmitri Mendeleev's periodic table of the elements simplified learning about chemistry.

2. Chemists at the First International Chemical Congress agreed on how to measure atomic weight.

3. Mendeleev predicted the properties of elements that filled gaps in the periodic table.

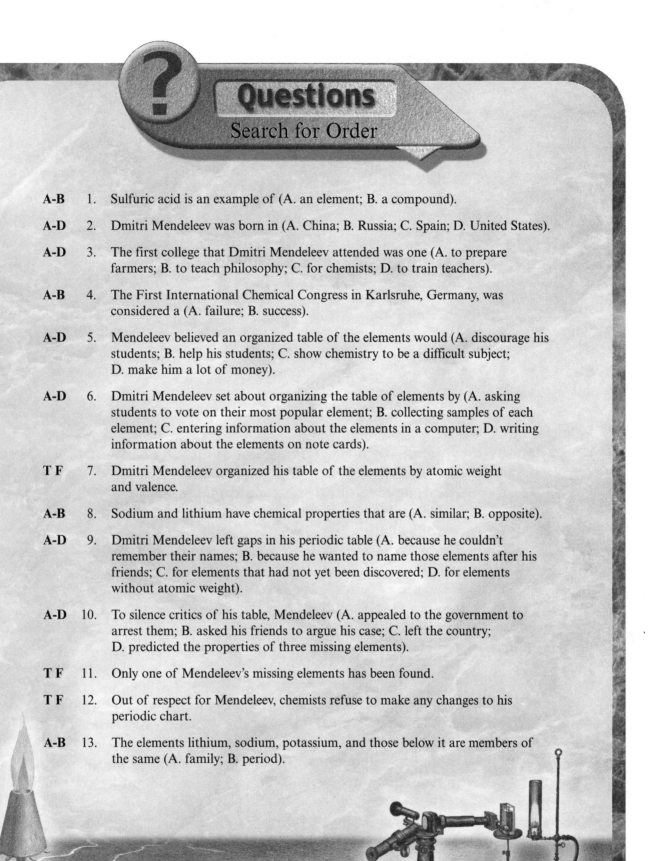

A-B   1.   Sulfuric acid is an example of (A. an element; B. a compound).

A-D   2.   Dmitri Mendeleev was born in (A. China; B. Russia; C. Spain; D. United States).

A-D   3.   The first college that Dmitri Mendeleev attended was one (A. to prepare farmers; B. to teach philosophy; C. for chemists; D. to train teachers).

A-B   4.   The First International Chemical Congress in Karlsruhe, Germany, was considered a (A. failure; B. success).

A-D   5.   Mendeleev believed an organized table of the elements would (A. discourage his students; B. help his students; C. show chemistry to be a difficult subject; D. make him a lot of money).

A-D   6.   Dmitri Mendeleev set about organizing the table of elements by (A. asking students to vote on their most popular element; B. collecting samples of each element; C. entering information about the elements in a computer; D. writing information about the elements on note cards).

T F   7.   Dmitri Mendeleev organized his table of the elements by atomic weight and valence.

A-B   8.   Sodium and lithium have chemical properties that are (A. similar; B. opposite).

A-D   9.   Dmitri Mendeleev left gaps in his periodic table (A. because he couldn't remember their names; B. because he wanted to name those elements after his friends; C. for elements that had not yet been discovered; D. for elements without atomic weight).

A-D 10.   To silence critics of his table, Mendeleev (A. appealed to the government to arrest them; B. asked his friends to argue his case; C. left the country; D. predicted the properties of three missing elements).

T F 11.   Only one of Mendeleev's missing elements has been found.

T F 12.   Out of respect for Mendeleev, chemists refuse to make any changes to his periodic chart.

A-B 13.   The elements lithium, sodium, potassium, and those below it are members of the same (A. family; B. period).

Sunlight Shows the Way

Chemists of the 1800s searched for new elements and sought to understand chemical properties. Three tools came to their aid in this quest. Electricity was one of the tools. Davy used it to discover sodium and other metallic elements. Mendeleev's periodic law was the second tool. With it, he predicted missing elements.

The third tool was the spectroscope. Like the flame test, the spectroscope uses light to reveal the elements hidden in a substance. The flame test only works with a few compounds. A spectroscope works with all substances.

Through a spectroscope, each element emits bands of light that identify it as exactly as fingerprints or DNA identify human beings. Chemists can learn the elements in an unknown

ACTION

1. A prism separated clear, white light into a rainbow of colors.

2. The spectrum of the sun was crossed by a series of lines.

3. Lines in the sun's spectrum could not be matched with any known element.

4. The inert gases did not fit into gaps in the periodic table.

Can You Predict the Reactions?

compound. They heat the substance until it glows and view the light through a spectroscope. Every element in the compound gives itself away by the light it emits.

The spectroscope did not suddenly appear on the scene. No one person can take full credit for its invention. Instead, several scientists over two hundred years had a role in its final form.

Isaac Newton, the English scientist, made the first contribution. He attended college at Cambridge, England. In 1666 the school closed because of an outbreak of the Black Death. Isaac fled to his home in the country. In the next 18 months, he investigated several of the unanswered questions of his day.

One question concerned the rainbow. The rainbow was a sign of the promise given by God to Noah and his family after the flood. (Read Genesis 9:13–17.)

Water droplets fill the air right after a rain. When sunlight passes through droplets of water, it breaks into a rainbow of colors. Where do the colors come from?

Isaac Newton darkened a room. He let in a small beam of sunlight through a hole in the window shutter. The ray passed through a prism that casts a rainbow upon a screen. A prism is a triangular piece of glass. Like raindrops, it separates sunlight into the familiar colors of the rainbow: red, orange, yellow, green, blue, and violet. These colors are known as the spectrum.

Some scientists believed that the colors did not exist in sunlight. They argued that sunlight, which they called white light, was pure and colorless. They insisted, "The glass colors the light as it passes through the prism."

Isaac disagreed. A glass prism was perfectly clear. So were raindrops. They couldn't add colors. He proved his point by passing the rainbow through a second prism turned to the reverse of the first. The colors recombined to cast a spot of

Isaac Newton with his prism

white light on the screen. All the colors of the rainbow go into making sunlight, or any white light that looks colorless. Rather than being without color, white light has all the colors in equal amounts.

Astronomers tried Newton's experiment with starlight. A prism hooked to a telescope spread starlight into the colors of the spectrum. Other than being dimmer, starlight was identical to sunlight. This convinced astronomers that stars are like the sun, but farther away.

The next advance was made by Joseph von Fraunhofer. Born March 6, 1787, of Straubing, Bavaria (Germany), Joseph wanted to study science, but his family was poor. They lived in an old and sagging apartment building. In the early 1800s, young children often worked in factories. Instead of studying science, Joseph labored in a glazing factory. For ten hours a day, he pushed trays of clay bowls and vases into a hot furnace.

One morning the old apartment building in which he lived crashed down without warning. His family was killed and Joseph was trapped in the rubble. The owner of an optical factory had his carriage blocked by the rescue effort. When workmen pulled the boy from the collapsed building, the factory owner

Joseph von Fraunhofer

took Joseph to the doctor. "All he needs is rest and a good meal," the doctor said.

After seeing to the boy's immediate needs, the businessman offered Joseph a job at the optical factory. At age 12 Joseph began grinding and polishing glass into lenses for telescopes and microscopes. The factory made prisms, also.

Joseph Fraunhofer proved himself at the optical company. He developed ways to make higher quality glass and better instruments. The factory owner rewarded his efforts. Joseph earned many promotions. Finally, the owner put Joseph in charge of the entire factory. Joseph became an expert at designing precision optical instruments. Astronomers valued his telescopes.

As a final quality check, Joseph Fraunhofer would test the optical equipment he built. In 1814 he looked through a new prism at a sodium flame. He noticed some bright lines across the spectrum. Was the prism defective? No, he tested other prisms. The lines were visible in good quality prisms but became fuzzy and difficult to detect in poor quality glass.

Fraunhofer continued to look for the lines. While testing prisms attached to telescopes, he counted 600 of the lines in the sun's spectrum. He made a chart of their position. They

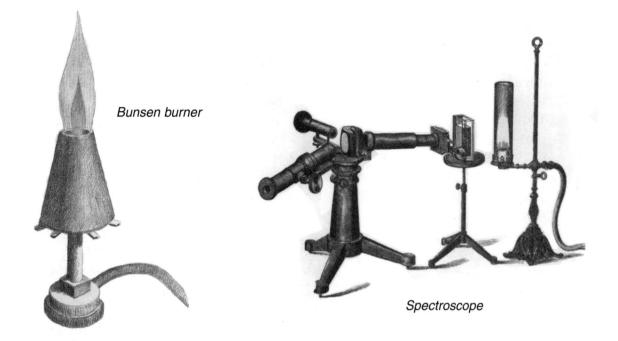

Bunsen burner

Spectroscope

always fell at the same place along the spectrum regardless of the source of the light. Fraunhofer questioned scientists as to the reason for the lines. They ignored his question, thinking it of no importance. He attended scientific meetings. Those who conducted the meetings did not allow him to speak. He had no formal education. He'd graduated from no famous school. He was, they thought, a mere technician who ground and polished glasses into useful shapes.

Joseph Fraunhofer died of tuberculosis in 1826 at the relatively young age of 39. Had he lived longer he might have convinced astronomers to study the dark lines more thoroughly.

Twenty-five years passed.

In the 1850s, Robert Bunsen taught chemistry at Heidelberg University. He had designed a burner that produced a hot, steady flame. His simple design mixed air with natural gas as a fuel. The burner had several advantages. It burned cleanly and did not release smoke. Chemists found it especially useful for the flame test. Soon, Bunsen burners were common fixtures in chemical laboratories everywhere.

Robert Bunsen believed he could improve upon the flame test. He asked a fellow teacher, Gustav Kirchhoff, for help. Gustav Kirchhoff admired Isaac Newton. He knew of Newton's work with prisms. He suggested that Bunsen view the flame through a prism.

Together, the two investigators built the first spectroscope. A prism spread the light into a broad band of colors.

Demonstrating the spectroscope

With a movable arm attached to a pointer they could read the exact position of a line in the spectrum.

A spectrum could have bright or dark lines. If the heated substance was hotter than its background, then the spectrum was a series of colored lines. Most substances in the laboratory produced bright-colored lines against a dark background. If the heated substance was against a still hotter background, then the lines would be dark. Dark lines crossed the sun's spectrum. Glowing gases in the sun's atmosphere were not as hot as its surface.

Whether bright or dark, the lines guided one to the element. In the spectroscope, each element produced its own signature, an arrangement of lines shared by no other element.

Sodium, for instance, glows with a pair of yellow lines close together. No other element produces lines exactly like those of sodium. Suppose a chemist has an unknown substance. He heats it until it glows and looks at the light with a spectroscope. If he sees sodium's two yellow lines, then he knows the unknown substance has sodium in it.

The spectroscope was a powerful tool. Suppose a glowing substance emitted lines unlike any others. Then the

Fraunhofer's achromatic refractor

substance must contain an unknown element.

In 1860, Bunsen and Kirchhoff used the spectroscope to search for new elements. They detected lines of sky blue unlike anything they had ever seen before. They named the element cesium from a Latin word meaning "sky blue." Cesium was the first element discovered by the spectroscope. The next year they found another new element. It had magnificent red lines in its spectrum. They called it rubidium from a Latin word which means "deep red."

Astronomers put a spectroscope on a telescope. They studied the lines in the sun's spectrum. As they had suspected, elements on earth also existed on the sun. Hydrogen, carbon, oxygen, nitrogen, iron, and many others revealed themselves by the light they emitted.

In 1868, Joseph Norman Lockyer matched the lines in the sun's spectrum against all known elements. One pattern did not match any known element. It was a particularly simple pattern. He concluded that the light came from an unknown element, possibly one that did not exist on earth. He named the new substance helium. The name means "from the sun."

The spectroscope also revealed a whole family of hidden elements. The elements were the noble family of gases. The noble family includes helium, neon, argon, krypton xenon, and radon. Despite staying hidden for so long, some of them are not particularly rare. Argon, for instance, makes up one percent of the atmosphere. They do not take part in chemical reaction. For that reason they escaped detection until the invention of the spectroscope.

The first hint that elements were in hiding came in 1785. Henry Cavendish (the English scientist who had found hydrogen) experimented with nitrogen from the atmosphere. Nitrogen is relatively inert. Although oxygen and nitrogen atoms are close to one another in the atmosphere, they do not normally combine. Cavendish sent an electric spark through a sample of air to force nitrogen and oxygen into chemical union.

A tiny bubble of air resisted the electric spark. Cavendish had an inspiration. Maybe the final bubble wasn't nitrogen. Maybe it was an element so inert the electric spark could not remove it. As usual, Cavendish moved on to another problem and did not fully report this experiment. In the 1870s his notes were rediscovered. Only then did chemists learn of the gas that refused to take part in chemical reactions.

In the 1890s, William Rayleigh, another Englishman, prepared nitrogen by releasing it from nitrogen compounds. These samples contained pure nitrogen. Next, Rayleigh took a sample of air and removed all known gases except nitrogen. He removed oxygen as well as water vapor, carbon dioxide, and all other known gases. With everything taken out, he should have had only nitrogen left.

Rayleigh took two equal volumes of each sample and weighed them. If both were pure nitrogen, they would weigh the same. The sample of nitrogen from the air weighed more than the sample of nitrogen generated from nitrogen compounds.

What could explain the difference in weight? Rayleigh tested various possibilities without success. In 1892, Rayleigh described his experiment in a scientific journal and asked for suggestions.

William Ramsay was a young Scottish chemist at University College, London. He had spent a year in Heidelberg working under the direction of Robert Bunsen. Bunsen had trained Ramsay in the use of the spectroscope. Ramsay wrote to Rayleigh and asked if he could work on the problem. Ramsay repeated Rayleigh's experiments and eliminated all possible solutions except one — the atmosphere contained a gas even more inert than nitrogen. Some other gas, heavier than nitrogen, remained mixed with it. The hidden gas made the sample heavier than pure nitrogen.

Ramsay kept in daily communication with Rayleigh. The telephone made it possible for them to work together although they were in separate laboratories. Ramsay applied the spectroscope to the problem. He isolated a bubble of the heavy air. Ramsay heated gas from the atmosphere and studied the lines of light it emitted. He found bright lines in a position that fitted no known element.

In 1894, Ramsay and Rayleigh announced the important discovery. "We've found a new element. It is a gas and one that is completely inert." The gas made up about one percent of the earth's atmosphere. It had no tendency to combine chemically with other elements. Ramsay named the gas argon, from a Greek word for "inert." It was a good name because argon has never been found to form any compounds.

Argon is colorless, tasteless, odorless, and nontoxic. Chemically, argon does nothing. What purpose can it serve? The first person who found a use for it was the great American inventor Thomas Alva Edison. He invented the first practical electric light bulb. When the filament of the bulb became hot enough to glow, the metal atoms boiled away. Every hour of use weakened the filament until it burned through. The first bulbs burned for only 40 hours. Edison prolonged the life by filling the bulb with a gas that exerted a pressure to keep the atoms of the white-hot filament from boiling away. At first, he used

Thomas Edison

nitrogen. Then in 1915 he switched to the even more inert argon.

The source of argon is the atmosphere. Air is chilled until the gases become a liquid. Then the temperature is raised and each gas boils off at a different temperature. Nitrogen boils first at -196°C (-321°F), followed by argon at -186°C (-303°F) and then oxygen at -183°C (-297°F).

Ramsay realized that argon was only one of an entire new family of elements. He began to search for the other members of the family. Ramsay had heard of a gas found above oil wells in the United States. He sent for a sample. Ramsay thought the gas might be his recently discovered argon. Instead, when the sample arrived, its spectr oscope lines matched exactly those lines Lockyer had noted in sunlight. Lockyer had found helium in the sun 27 years before Ramsay found it on earth.

In 1898, Ramsay chilled a sample of the atmosphere until it turned into a liquid. He warmed the liquid air and captured gases as they boiled off.

The Edison light bulb

He discovered three gases by this method and named them neon ("new"), krypton ("hidden"), and xenon ("stranger"). Two years later he investigated a gas emitted by radioactive radium. The gas, named radon, was the last in the new family of elements.

Chemists called the new gases inert ("no action") and noble ("aloof") gases. Left to themselves they do not form compounds with other elements. For that reason, chemists give them a valence of zero.

Where do they fit in the periodic table? An element missing here or there left a hole in the table. Chemists could see those holes and predict missing elements. No one suspected an entire family of missing elements. No chemist predicted the existence of the inert gases. Their discovery did not destroy the periodic table. Instead, they completed it. On most periodic tables, the inert gases are shown as an a vertical family to the right of the chlorine family.

Although the inert gases have practically no use in chemical compounds, they do have many other uses.

Helium, like hydrogen, is lighter than air. Helium doesn't explode when mixed with air or oxygen. During the 1920s and 1930s, America filled its blimps and dirigibles with helium. Today, the only reminders of the great airships are a few helium-filled advertising blimps. Meteorologists also inflate sounding balloons with helium to carry scientific packages high into the atmosphere.

The primary use for neon is in neon lights. When a high voltage electric current passes through any gas at low pressure, the gas glows. The color of the glow is the same as the gas's spectral lines when viewed through a spectroscope.

Neon glows red. Krypton glows a brilliant green. Xenon emits a blue light. Eye-catching advertising signs use inert gases to fill the tubes. People call them neon signs, although they may contain any of the inert gases.

Krypton, Kr, received its name from the Greek word *kryptos* meaning "hidden." Back in the 1930s, two young artists began the Superman comic strip.

Xenon is used to create a camera's flash.

They chose krypton as a scientific sounding name for Superman's home planet. They also imagined a mineral, kryptonite, that gave off radiation harmful to Superman. In real life, there is an element krypton but no mineral kryptonite.

When a high voltage discharge zaps xenon, the gas produces an intense, brilliant flash of light. Cameras have flashes for taking pictures in low light. A camera's flash has a tube of xenon gas. Xenon strobe lights serve as beacons on airport runways and to mark the tops of high buildings.

Are the inert gases truly inert? Chemists thought so for more than 50 years. In 1962, Neil Bartlett researched the question. To his surprise, he found that no chemist had attempted to make inert gas compounds.

Neil Bartlett was a chemist at the University of British Columbia. He heated a mixture of xenon gas and fluorine gas with fine particles of platinum inside a container made of nickel. When he finished the experiment he found a tiny purple crystal of xenon, fluorine, and platinum. The crystal was stable at room temperature in dry air. When touched, the crystal disappeared with a pop due to a reaction with moisture from the skin.

This was a startling discovery. Bartlett's choices for the reaction were logical. He knew heat helped reactions along. The metal nickel served as a catalyst. (A catalyst promotes a chemical reaction without actually being consumed in the reaction itself.) Fluorine is the most active element known, even more active than oxygen. Chemists could have done the experiment years earlier, but no one had thought to do so. Everybody believed that the inert gases formed no compounds.

Later Bartlett made a simpler compound containing only xenon and oxygen (xenon trioxide, XeO_3). Chemists also make compounds with krypton. However, compounds of the lighter inert gases — argon, neon, and helium — have never been formed.

The spectroscope helped chemists fill in the periodic chart. By the end of the 1800s, efforts of chemists turned more to studying chemical compounds. Before they could make real progress, they had to understand the role of the electron in chemical reactions. They could do this only after they learned what was inside the atom itself.

REACTION

1. Sunlight had all the colors in equal amounts.

2. Each element in the sun revealed itself by the lines in the spectrum.

3. Helium was detected by its spectrum in the sun before it was found on earth.

4. The inert gases completed the periodic table as a separate chemical family.

A-D 1. The three most important tools for making advances in chemistry were electricity, the periodic law, and the (A. law of buoyancy; B. microscope; C. spectroscope; D. telescope).

A-B 2. Isaac Newton proved that white light from the sun (A. is pure light without colors; B. contains all the colors of the rainbow).

A-D 3. Joseph von Fraunhofer (A. died in the collapse of an apartment building; B. worked as a child in a factory that glazed pottery; C. studied chemistry in a well-equipped home laboratory; D. was the son of a nobleman).

T F 4. Fraunhofer saw the lines in the spectrum while testing the quality of a prism.

T F 5. Joseph Fraunhofer invented the spectroscope in 1826 following a lecture he gave to a group of scientists.

T F 6. Robert Bunsen invented the Bunsen burner.

A-D 7. The first element discovered by the spectroscope was (A. cesium; B. helium; C. kryptonite; D. uranium).

T F 8. Helium was discovered on the sun before it was discovered on earth.

A-D 9. Henry Cavendish combined oxygen with nitrogen by using (A. an electric spark; B. high heat; C. intense cold; D. great pressure).

T F 10. When Rayleigh weighed equal volumes of nitrogen freed from compounds with nitrogen separated from the atmosphere, they weighed the same.

T F 11. In 1892, Rayleigh announced that his experiment revealed a new element in the atmosphere.

A-D 12. Argon makes up about (A. 1; B. 5; C. 78; D. 21) percent of the atmosphere of the earth.

T F 13. Argon helps make light bulbs last longer.

A-D 14. The name helium means from (A. Helena, Montana; B. the hills; C. the sun; D. uranium).

A-D 15. The noble gas family is also known as the (A. empire of the sun family; B. inert gases; C. Ramsay and Rayleigh family; D. strange family).

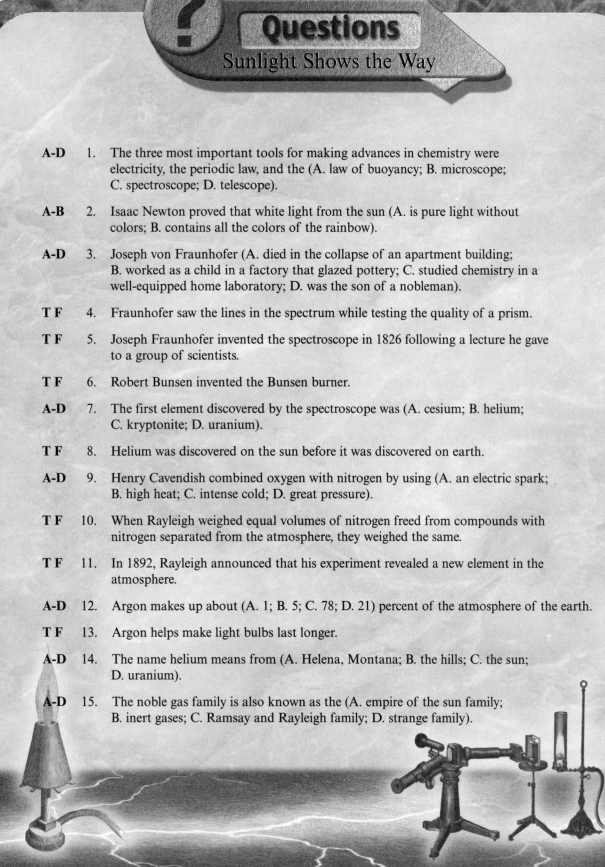

The Electron Shows the Way

Chemists eagerly used the spectroscope to examine the bright lines of new elements. However, they struggled to understand what caused the colors. One element radiated yellow light. Another element radiated violet light. Why?

Chemists also wondered about the periodic law. What caused sodium and its family to have a valence of one? Explanations were needed for other mysteries, too. For instance, when electricity flowed through water, hydrogen bubbled up around the negative terminal but oxygen bubbled up around the positive terminal. Why the difference? Why did elements differ in the chemical combining power? It took two atoms of sodium to combine with oxygen, but only one atom of calcium. What caused the atom to react differently?

During the 1800s, chemists uncovered all the clues they needed to solve the mysteries.

ACTION

1. Elements differed in the way they combined with other elements.

2. A simple battery of copper, zinc, and sulfuric acid generated electricity.

3. Chemists needed to probe inside an atom to learn its structure and composition.

Can You Predict the Reactions?

Some scientists believed matter to be continuous. They believed they could divide and subdivide a lump of gold endlessly. They would never come to a smallest particle of gold. Others believed that matter is made of atoms. At some stage the dividing would give a particle of gold that could not be divided any further and still be gold.

In the early 1800s, John Dalton showed that the second view of matter was correct. John Dalton was a Quaker who received an education from his father, a weaver. He attended a Quaker school. After he graduated at age 11, he returned the next year as a teacher. He was younger than some of his students. Later, he became the mathematics and science teacher at a college in Manchester, England. In the early 1800s, England's best universities were Oxford and Cambridge. Only students who attended the Church of England could attend those schools. The college in Manchester opened its doors to students who did not belong to the Church of England.

John Dalton was entirely self-taught in science. One of his first scientific successes was a study of weather. Weather had always interested him. He built his own weather gauges and kept a daily weather journal. Throughout his life, he recorded more than 200,000 entries. He studied the atmosphere and other gases. He showed that falling temperature rather than a change in air pressure caused clouds to release their burden of rain.

Dalton could best explain the properties

John Dalton

of air by supposing that air was made of tiny particles. He became convinced that all elements are composed of tiny, indestructible particles. Matter, he said, was made of atoms. The word atom was from a Greek word meaning "incapable of being cut."

According to Dalton's atomic theory, atoms of the same element were identical in all their properties, including their weight. Atoms of different elements differed from one another, especially in their weight. For instance, hydrogen is made of atoms that are all alike. Oxygen is made of atoms, too. But the oxygen atoms differ from the hydrogen atoms. One property of oxygen atoms is that they are 16 times heavier than hydrogen atoms.

Dalton's atomic theory also predicted that atoms combine in ratios of simple whole numbers. For instance, hydrogen and oxygen atoms combine in the ratio of 2 to 1. Water is H_2O, which means two atoms of hydrogen combine with one atom of oxygen. Atoms always combine in whole numbers in exactly the same way. A water molecule always has exactly two hydrogen atoms and one oxygen atom. It cannot have 1.5 or 2.5 hydrogen atoms because atoms cannot be divided during chemical reactions.

John Dalton announced his atomic theory in 1803. His ideas were not idle speculation but were based on experimental evidence. The theory was quickly accepted and soon became a foundation of modern chemistry.

For most of his life, John Dalton earned a living as a teacher and tutor. He was a humble Quaker who did not seek personal fame. Once, friends arranged for him to meet King William IV of England. However, to do so he would have to wear richly colored court dress that included a ceremonial sword. Quakers could not carry weapons and avoided showy clothing. He declined the meeting rather than violate his religious beliefs. Later, he received a doctor's degree from Oxford. The king would receive him in the official Oxford cap and gown. The robe had no sword. Although it was a bright scarlet, John Dalton wore it. He was color-blind and to him it appeared a dull gray.

Atoms are the smallest objects that have the chemical properties of an element. However, they are not the smallest bits of matter. Still smaller particles make the atom. Even as Dalton announced his atomic theory, chemists puzzled about electricity. Was it a continuous fluid? Or, was electricity made of particles, too? More importantly, what role did electricity play in chemical reactions?

Humphry Davy had shown that electricity could separate atoms in compounds. Electricity disrupted the attraction between atoms and caused a molecule to come apart. He separated sodium from soda ash by electricity. Although chemists did not understand the reason, they knew the electricity caused sodium and oxygen in soda ash to separate.

For that matter, how can chemicals generate electricity? A simple battery has two electrodes such as copper and zinc in a solution of sulfuric acid. When the circuit is complete, electricity flows. What puts the electricity in motion?

These questions were partially answered in the late 1800s by an amateur scientist named William Crookes.

William Crookes had inherited a large fortune. He could do whatever he wanted. What he enjoyed most was scientific experimentation. He built his own private laboratory in London. He mastered the use of the spectroscope. In 1861 he saw a beautiful green line in the spectrum of a metallic ore. The line fitted no other element. He named the new metal thallium from a Greek word meaning "green twig." Thallium, Tl, is a poisonous metallic element as is lead, its neighbor in the periodic table.

Crookes refined a small sample of his new element thallium. To measure its atomic weight, he put the tiny sample in a balance pan. To keep air currents from upsetting the scale, he put the balance in a vacuum chamber. However, the balance never did settle down. The pans jittered up and down in tiny irregular motions.

Crookes knew that a perfect vacuum was impossible. Even the best vacuum chamber still has a few stray air molecules in it. Were the molecules bouncing around and striking the pans? Would the molecules of air have enough energy to move the pans?

To test the idea, Crookes invented the radiometer. This simple device converted sunlight into motion. A radiometer looked like a clear glass light bulb with a weathervane inside. The weathervane

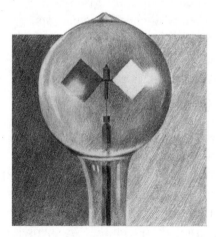

Radiometer

balanced on a pin and was free to turn. He painted one side of each vane black. He painted the other side of each vane white. He removed most of the air and sealed the globe. The side of the vane painted black absorbed sunlight and got warm. It warmed nearby air molecules. They struck the vanes and caused the pinwheel to turn.

William Crookes' invention was very sensitive. Crookes focused starlight from a telescope on the vanes. The pinwheel turned from the heating effect of faint starlight. For many years, the radiometer was used to measure the strength of radiant energy. Radiant energy is energy from heat or light. Instruments that are more sensitive have since replaced it. Radiometers are still sold in children's toy stores and science shops.

During these tests William Crookes became an expert at using an air pump to remove the air from a container. He took a glass tube with electrodes at each end. He removed the air from the tube and tried to send electricity through the vacuum. Invisible rays shot out from the negative end of the tube. They traveled the length of the tube and struck the other end, causing a steady greenish glow.

Crooke's tube became known as a cathode ray tube, abbreviated CRT.

The negative terminal was known as the cathode. Crookes' tube became known as a cathode ray tube, abbreviated CRT. What were the rays? Experimentation showed that they were particles smaller than the atom. They carried a negative charge. They were later named electrons.

Electric and magnetic fields on either side of the tube could control the flight of the electrons. Inventors used the cathode ray tube for a variety of purposes. The stream of electrons painted glowing trails across a screen and provided a visual image of a changing electric current. Electricians repaired circuits by studying the changing current as displayed on a special CRT known as an oscilloscope.

Although the cathode ray tube is more than a hundred years old, modified versions of it are still in daily use. CRTs in hospitals trace out heart activity and other vital signs of patients. The moving image of a television is actually a series of still images. Electric and magnetic fields control the stream of electrons to paint 30 images a second on a television picture tube. Many computer monitors and electronic games use cathode ray tubes for presenting information to the user.

Some people, as they grow older, become set in their ways and refuse to learn new information. William Crookes kept the enthusiasm of his youth. Even as an old man, young chemistry students came to him for his ideas about how to solve their problems. William Ramsay asked Crookes for help in identifying the inert gases.

Chemists began investigating the electron. They soon found that it was far lighter than a hydrogen atom. It takes 1,837 electrons to weigh as much as a single hydrogen atom. This is proof that they are smaller than an atom. Further tests showed that all elements contain electrons. Atoms, the building blocks of matter, are themselves composed of smaller building blocks.

Atoms are electrically neutral. Chemists realized atoms must also contain positive charges to balance the negative charge of electrons. How was the positive charge arranged? Most chemists imagined the atom as a sticky glob of positive material with the negative electrons embedded in it. This picture became known as the "plum pudding model" of the atom.

How could one see into the atom? Imagine standing outside a darkened room. You can only throw balls into the room and from the way they bounce around learn about the furnishings in the room. The atom was like the dark room. Chemists needed an atomic ball to send into the atom. From how the ball bounced around they would learn about what made the atom and how electrons were arranged.

In 1906 Ernest Rutherford found the right atomic ball to bounce against atoms. Although born in New Zealand, he came to Cambridge, England to study. He was a big man, but had an unusual ability to do delicate experiments with tiny subjects. He investigated emission from radioactive elements such as uranium and radium. Alpha rays were a mysterious form of radiation given off by radioactive elements. Rutherford showed that alpha rays were particles. They traveled about 20,000 miles per second, more than one-tenth of the speed of light. They were about four times as heavy as a hydrogen atom. They carried a

positive electric charge.

Ernest Rutherford realized that alpha particles would serve for probing the inside of an atom. With their high speed and mass, they would cut deep into the atom.

Rutherford used gold as his subject. Gold is the most malleable of metals. Goldsmiths can hammer it into exceedingly thin sheets. Rutherford used gold foil so thin that fifty thousand layers of it would only be an inch thick. Atoms are incredibly tiny. Even so, Rutherford's foil was only two thousand atoms thick.

Rutherford fired alpha particles into the gold foil. On the other side, he watched a screen. As each alpha particle struck the screen, it made a brief flash of light. Rutherford expected the alpha particles to hit the massive gold atoms and bounce around. The alpha particles entered as a straight stream on one side of the foil. He expected them to come out in all directions on the other side.

Much to Rutherford's surprise, most alpha particles passed straight through the foil. Gold is a heavy metal. The alpha particles passed through the foil as easily as a bullet through tissue paper.

As the experiment continued, gold atoms did bump a few alpha particles off course. Even more surprising, about 1 in 10,000 alpha particles bounced right back out. Rather than hitting empty space, they'd hit something remarkably solid. Ernest Rutherford sat back, astonished. How could he explain these observations?

Rutherford announced his picture of the atom. It differed a lot from the solid plum pudding model. According to

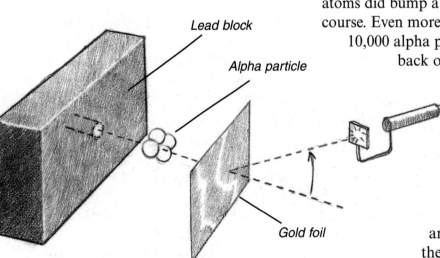

Diagram of alpha particle experiment

Lead block

Alpha particle

Gold foil

Rutherford, atoms were mostly empty space. The material was not spread evenly throughout the atom. Instead, its mass was concentrated in a dense, central core. The core, called the nucleus, was both tiny and heavy. An alpha particle bounced back only when it hit the nucleus dead center. Most alpha particles missed the nucleus entirely and kept right on going.

Swarming around the nucleus were electrons with a negative charge. They were very light. Alpha particles brushed them aside as if they didn't exist. Because only 1 in 10,000 alpha particles struck the nucleus, Rutherford believed the nucleus was 1/10,000th the diameter of the entire atom.

Rutherford's description of the atom is called the "planetary model" of the atom. The nucleus corresponds to the sun and the electrons to the planets.

In 1920, Rutherford suggested that the smallest positive particle would be the hydrogen atom with its electron removed. He gave the name proton to this single positive charge. The word proton is Greek meaning "the first."

The electric charge of a proton is positive. The electric charge of an electron is negative. The two charges are equal in size. They exactly cancel one another. However, an electron and proton do differ in mass. A proton is 1,836 times as heavy as an electron.

The positive charges of the protons balance the negative charges of the electrons. For instance, carbon has six protons. Normally, it has six electrons. The six positive charges from the protons cancel the six negative electric charges from the electrons.

Carbon atom

Overall, the atom is electrically neutral.

Rutherford's discovery convinced chemists that atoms contain both protons and electrons. Later, in 1932, James Chadwick discovered that atoms have a third particle, a neutron. The neutron is about the same mass as a proton, but it has no electric charge. It is electrically neutral, which explains its name. Protons and neutrons squeeze tightly together in the nucleus.

With this understanding, Rutherford realized that an alpha particle was identical to a high-speed helium nucleus.

Atoms are incredibly tiny. A million atoms put side by side would be less than the width of a human hair. An atom is mostly empty space. Suppose you could magnify a gold atom to fill a football stadium. It would still be difficult to see. At the center of the field would be the nucleus, no bigger than a marble. Flying around at the top seats in the stadium would be a hazy cloud of electrons.

With this model of the atom, so much about chemistry became easier to understand. An electric current is merely the flow of electrons. In metals such as copper and silver, some electrons orbit at the outer fringes of the atom. The atom loosely holds them. They can drift away. Electrons weigh little and move readily. What flows through a copper wire is not a mysterious fluid but millions of electrons.

Electrons explained the unique light given off by each element. Each element has its electrons arranged in regions around the nucleus. Electrons absorb light as they gain energy. They emit light as they lose energy. No two elements have electrons arranged in exactly the same way. The electrons of each element produce a different display of light. Each element has its own series of lines as seen in the spectrum. The lines are light if the gas is hot and glowing. The lines are dark if the gas is cool and against a brighter background.

Electrons explain chemical combining power (valence) of atoms. Elements discard, accept, or share electrons to become more stable. The inert elements have a valence of zero because they already have their electrons in a stable arrangement. They are unlikely to take part in chemical reactions because they have no need to gain, lose, or share electrons.

For instance, the inert gas neon has ten electrons. Two electrons orbit near the nucleus and the other eight orbit farther out. Sodium has eleven electrons. Ten of the electrons are in a pattern similar to the electrons in neon. However, sodium has one additional electron orbiting far away from the nucleus. If sodium could get rid of that electron, it would have the stable

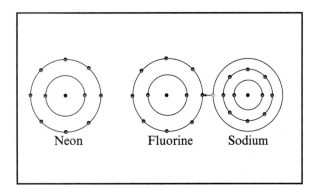

Neon   Fluorine   Sodium

electron arrangement of neon. Sodium is willing to give up that electron, which is why it has a valence of one.

Fluorine has nine electrons. If it could gain one electron, it would have the stable electron arrangement of neon. Fluorine

is willing to accept an electron to meet its more stable goal. Should a sodium atom and a fluorine atom come near one another, an electron exchange is likely. Sodium wants to give up an electron and fluorine wants to accept an electron. A chemical reaction is simply what happens when atoms meet to rearrange their electrons.

What is the role of the electron in chemistry? All chemical reactions involve electrons. Chemical reactions take place whenever atoms gain, lose, or share electrons. With this understanding of the electron, chemists could investigate chemical compounds with a new understanding.

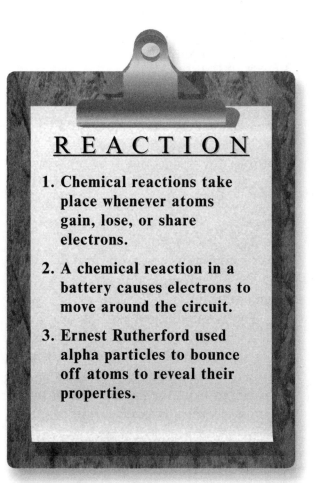

REACTION

1. **Chemical reactions take place whenever atoms gain, lose, or share electrons.**

2. **A chemical reaction in a battery causes electrons to move around the circuit.**

3. **Ernest Rutherford used alpha particles to bounce off atoms to reveal their properties.**

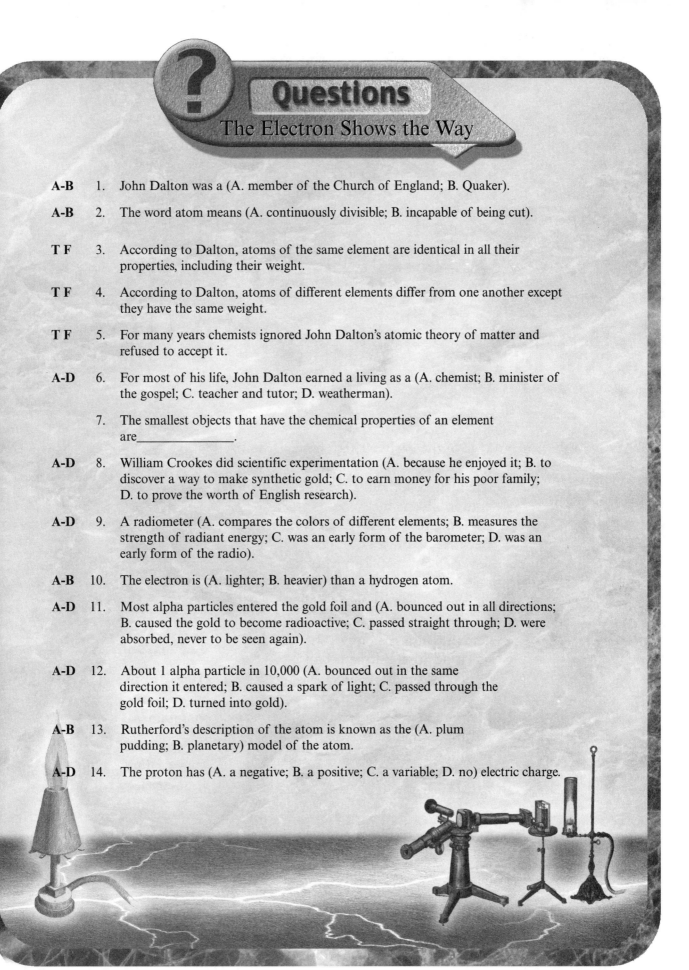

A-B 1. John Dalton was a (A. member of the Church of England; B. Quaker).

A-B 2. The word atom means (A. continuously divisible; B. incapable of being cut).

T F 3. According to Dalton, atoms of the same element are identical in all their properties, including their weight.

T F 4. According to Dalton, atoms of different elements differ from one another except they have the same weight.

T F 5. For many years chemists ignored John Dalton's atomic theory of matter and refused to accept it.

A-D 6. For most of his life, John Dalton earned a living as a (A. chemist; B. minister of the gospel; C. teacher and tutor; D. weatherman).

7. The smallest objects that have the chemical properties of an element are_____.

A-D 8. William Crookes did scientific experimentation (A. because he enjoyed it; B. to discover a way to make synthetic gold; C. to earn money for his poor family; D. to prove the worth of English research).

A-D 9. A radiometer (A. compares the colors of different elements; B. measures the strength of radiant energy; C. was an early form of the barometer; D. was an early form of the radio).

A-B 10. The electron is (A. lighter; B. heavier) than a hydrogen atom.

A-D 11. Most alpha particles entered the gold foil and (A. bounced out in all directions; B. caused the gold to become radioactive; C. passed straight through; D. were absorbed, never to be seen again).

A-D 12. About 1 alpha particle in 10,000 (A. bounced out in the same direction it entered; B. caused a spark of light; C. passed through the gold foil; D. turned into gold).

A-B 13. Rutherford's description of the atom is known as the (A. plum pudding; B. planetary) model of the atom.

A-D 14. The proton has (A. a negative; B. a positive; C. a variable; D. no) electric charge.

Compounds by Electrical Attraction

In the early 1900s, chemists realized that electrons have the main role in chemical reactions. One way atoms form compounds is by exchanging electrons. A sodium atom easily gives up an electron. Because of the loss, it has fewer electrons than protons and becomes electrically charged. Chemists write the charged sodium ion as Na^+. The plus sign, +, shows that it has a positive charge because it has lost an electron.

On the other side of the periodic table is the chlorine family of elements. An atom of chlorine readily accepts an electron. In doing so, it has more electrons than protons, so it has a negative charge. Chemists write the charged chlorine atom as Cl^-. The minus sign, -, shows that it has a negative charge because it has gained an electron.

The two charged atoms, Na^+ and Cl^-, have opposite

ACTION

1. Highly active elements have especially stable compounds.

2. Cities thrive in harsh, desert climates but cities in good climates failed.

3. Because it was so chemically active, fluorine resisted being freed from other elements.

Can You Predict the Reactions?

charges. As Benjamin Franklin's static electricity experiments showed, unlike charges attract. Sodium and chlorine ions attract one another because of their opposite electric charge. They form sodium chlorine, or table salt, $NaCl$. Because sodium and chlorine have equal but opposite charges, the combination of sodium and chlorine is electrically neutral.

The chlorine family has five elements: fluorine, F; chlorine, Cl; bromine, Br; iodine, I; and astatine, At. The family is noted for its strong chemical activity. All members of the chlorine family are too active chemically to be free in nature. In combination with other elements, they are abundant and found in a variety of common compounds, especially salts. The chlorine family is also known as the halogens, a word meaning "the salt makers."

The most common salt is ordinary table salt. Salt has been in use since ancient times. Salt is mentioned in Genesis 19:26 when Lot's wife is turned into a pillar of salt. Today, salt is an everyday substance, and we take no special notice of it. In ancient times, people had few sources of salt, so it was valuable. Caravans crossed vast distances to carry salt to large cities.

If a Roman soldier from ancient times could come to modern America following a winter storm, he would be surprised. He would see what he thought of as money being dumped on the streets. Today salt is cheap enough to spread on roads and sidewalks to melt ice. That was not true in ancient times.

Ancient people had fewer sources of salt so it was more highly prized. Roman soldiers received part of their pay in salt. The Roman word for salt, sal, is the root word for "salary." The value of salt is shown by the expression, "He is worth his salt." The expression refers to soldiers who earned the salary of salt.

The city of Ostia in Italy supplied salt to Rome by evaporating seawater from the Mediterranean Sea. Like the oceans, water from the Mediterranean Sea contained about three percent salt. After being led into shallow lakes, sunlight evaporated the water. The thick mixture of salt and water was drained into smaller pans for further drying. So important was Ostia to the Roman Empire that the highway to the sea was named Via Salarium, or the Road of Salt.

About 1,600 years ago, the sea level changed and flooded the salt beds at Ostia. Rome turned to another supply in the Middle East land of Israel: the Dead Sea. Although salt was far more concentrated in the Dead Sea, returning it to Rome was a greater chore.

Lot's wife

A caravan of a thousand camels each carrying 500 pounds of salt hauled it out.

For a long time, historians wondered why some cities thrived in harsh climates such as at the edge of deserts. Other cities in more favorable climates fell into ruin. They found that many civilizations developed near deserts because salt was plentiful. At the edge of the Sahara Desert in Africa, the city of Timbuktu survived because the desert supplied salt. Other cities could not find salt because frequent rains dissolved it. Salt disappeared into the ground or was washed away. Those cities without salt either died out or had to pay high prices for their salt.

Salt was so valuable in Bible times that people added clay to make it last longer. In the Bible, the salt which lost its saltiness (Matt. 5:13) was salt with clay or sand added. The clay was all that remained after the salt had been washed out.

Salt does more than flavor foods because humans require salt in their diets. Some of the necessary nutrients such as proteins will not dissolve in water alone. Salt helps dissolve the protein for blood to carry throughout the body.

Livestock and wild animals need salt just as

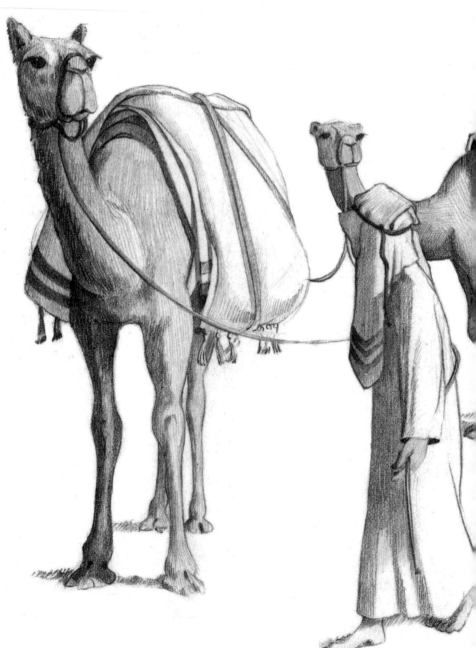

humans do. Farmers put salt blocks in the barnyard for their cattle. Ranchers drop salt blocks by airplane so their livestock will not have so far to travel to satisfy their need for the mineral. Deer and other wild animals travel to natural salt licks. A salt lick is soil that has a natural deposit of salt.

In Africa, explorers discovered a

cave that had been dug into the mountain. As they watched, elephants entered the cave and used their tusks to dig deeper into the natural salt formation. Elephants in search of salt had dug the cave to satisfy their need for salt.

Columbus began his trip of exploration to find a shorter route to the Orient where spices, including salt, could be bought. Instead, Columbus found the New World. Salt is abundant in some places in America. The Bonneville Salt Flats in Utah is a dried lakebed. This vast bed of salt extends for miles in every direction. It is so flat that automobiles set speed records on its surface. Often, salt deposits such as those in Utah are so pure the salt can be mined and bagged for shipment without any other treatment.

Look at a particle of ordinary table salt with a magnifying lens. All salts form crystals. Table salt crystals are cubes. Crystal patterns of other salts are different. This fact helps a chemist identify a salt by its crystalline shape.

Salt illustrates the fact that a compound can be harmless and beneficial while the elements that make it can be far different. Salt contains chlorine and sodium. Chlorine is a heavy, choking, green gas. Sodium is a soft silver-white metal that reacts violently with water. Both sodium and chlorine are poisonous. Salt, taken in moderation, is beneficial to the human diet.

Chlorine supports combustion. If you put a lighted candle into a container of pure chlorine, the flame continues to burn. Chlorine is an extremely active nonmetal. Only oxygen and fluorine are more active.

Chlorine reacts readily with carbon. All living things are made of carbon compounds. Chlorine attacks those compounds and destroys them. People often use chlorine to purify water and kill bacteria in swimming pools. With as few as ten chlorine atoms per million water

Caravans of camels carried salt back to Rome.

73

molecules, it kills most bacteria. It is harmless to humans in such small amounts.

Chlorinating drinking water to kill germs was first tried in 1897. An outbreak of typhoid fever struck London. Heath officials marked on a map of the city where the victims first came down with the sickness. They saw that the epidemic was clustered around public wells. London officials added chlorine to the public water supply to kill the germs and stop that highly infectious disease. They did their work secretly because some people objected to chemists tampering with the water.

When combined with hydrogen, chlorine produces hydrochloric acid, HCl. This strong acid is found in the human stomach where it helps in the digestion of food. Another strong acid is hydroflouric acid, HF. It is so powerful it will dissolve glass. It has to be stored in wax or plastic bottles because it would eat its way out of a glass bottle.

Salt crystal

One use of hydrofluoric acid is to etch designs into glass. The artist covers the sheet of glass with wax. Then the artist uses a blade to cut a design into the wax. Next, hydrofluoric acid is spread over the sheet and eats a cloudy pattern in the part of the glass not protected by the wax. Once the wax is removed, the artist has created a design in the glass.

Fluorine, F, is the lightest member of the chlorine family and the most reactive of all elements. Fluorine is a highly poisonous and a highly corrosive pale yellow gas. Fluorine is so reactive it will form compounds with almost all other elements. It will strip water apart to capture electrons.

Chemists have learned that reactive elements have stable compounds that are difficult to separate into individual atoms. Fluorine forms extremely stable compounds. Chemists of the 1800s had no samples of fluorine because it could not be found free in nature. It was locked tightly in its compounds. Freeing it was extremely difficult.

When they did succeed in freeing it, the gas promptly combined with anything nearby and disappeared before chemists could study it.

Success in producing uncombined fluorine came to French chemist Henri Moissan in 1886. (He would later be the victim of the hoax that made him think he had produced synthetic diamond.) He knew platinum to be an inert metal. So he correctly believed it would react only slightly with fluorine. Although platinum was more expensive than gold, he made his equipment from that metal. He chilled the apparatus to -50°C (-58°F) to reduce the activity of fluorine. He passed an electric current through a solution of potassium fluoride and hydrofluoric acid. The reaction released a pale yellow gas, the long sought-after fluorine.

Fluorine is found in minerals such as fluorite and cryolite. When struck by ultraviolet rays, fluorite crystals emit vivid fluorescent light. The effect is quite astonishing because the crystals seem to glow all by themselves. Actually, ultraviolet light, also known as black light, is invisible to human eyes. Fluorite changes the invisible rays to visible light. Many museums have dark rooms illuminated by ultraviolet light to show fluorite crystals.

Bromine, Br, is another member of the chlorine family. Bromine is one of only two elements that is a liquid at room temperature. (Mercury is the other.) Above liquid bromine, a beautiful but pungent-smelling red vapor gathers. The name bromine is from a Greek word meaning "stench," a reference to its powerful, unpleasant odor.

Sea plants and animals concentrate bromine in their bodies. The murex is a snail that lives in the Mediterranean Sea. It contains bromine compounds that can be used as a dye. Phoenicians used the murex to prepare Tyrian purple, a bromine dye of ancient times. It commanded high prices in the markets of Greece and Rome. The name Tyrian comes from the city of Tyre, a famous Phoenician trading port. When Solomon built the temple, the king of Tyre supplied him with some of his building materials. (See 1 Kings 9:11.) Jesus visited Tyre and Sidon (Matt. 15:21). Paul waited a week with fellow Christians in the city while his ship unloaded its cargo (Acts 21:3-7).

Henri Moissan

Today, ocean water is the primary source of bromine. Bromine is one of a few elements that can be removed from the sea at a profit. Bromine is an important chemical in photography. Silver bromide, AgBr, is highly sensitive to light. An emulsion containing silver bromide coats photographic paper and film. When exposed to light, the silver bromide carries a latent image. Photographers can then develop the hidden image.

A bromide is any combination of bromide with another element. Common bromines are potassium bromide, KBr, and sodium bromide, NaBr. For many years, people used bromides as sedatives to help them sleep.

Iodine, I, is a shiny, blue-black element. At room temperature, its crystals have a luster like a metal, although it is a nonmetal. People use iodine primarily for medical reasons. Tincture of iodine is alcohol with iodine dissolved in it. For a long time, tincture of iodine was a well-known and effective germ killer. Cuts were painted with the tincture of iodine to prevent harmful bacteria from entering the wound. It was so harsh it damaged the skin. Other antiseptics have replaced it.

A small amount of iodine is essential in the diet to insure proper functioning of the thyroid glands. Iodized salt contains

Iodine was used to prevent infection.

mostly sodium chloride, NaCl, but a small amount of potassium iodide, KI, is added to supply iodine in the diet.

Scientists have found that crystals containing iodine act as the core around which water vapor condenses out of clouds. For a time, silver iodide crystals were used to seed clouds in an attempt to promote rainfall. No one has yet proven that the seeding increased the total rainfall. Evidence does suggest that seeding clouds with silver iodide crystals changes where rain falls and how much falls in a local area. A more fruitful line of research is controlling fog. Chemists believe they can limit the formation of fog on airport runways and along busy highways prone to fog by spraying silver iodide crystals in the moist air.

REACTION

1. The ions have unlike charges and attract one another strongly.

2. Salt was necessary for survival but could be washed away by rain.

3. Henri Moissan made laboratory equipment of platinum to study fluorine.

A-D 1. The plus sign, +, for the charged sodium atom, Na^+, shows that it (A. carries a negative charge; B. has more protons than electrons; C. is made of a single proton; D. is too big to take part in chemical reaction).

A-D 2. The charged sodium atom, Na^+, and the charged chlorine atom, Cl^-, will (A. attract one another; B. come together and destroy one another; C. produce an electric current; D. repel one another).

A-D 3. Another name for the chlorine family is (A. acid makers; B. alkali makers; C. radioactive family; D. salt makers).

A-D 4. The Roman word for salt is the root word for (A. acid; B. dry; C. salary; D. seawater).

5. Timbuktu is located at the edge of the _____ Desert.

T F 6. Although salt flavors food, it has no other purpose in the diet.

A-D 7. Henri Moissan made his laboratory equipment of platinum because (A. he had money to spare; B. it becomes solid at extremely cold temperatures; C. it reacts only slightly with fluorine; D. it is a cheap metal).

A-C 8. At room temperature bromine is a (A. gas; B. liquid; C. solid).

A-B 9. Chlorinating drinking water was first tried in London in 1897 to (A. prevent tooth decay; B. stop an outbreak of typhoid fever).

A-D 10. The acid found in the stomach that helps digestion is (A. acetic; B. hydrochloric; C. hydrofluoric; D. sulfuric) acid.

11. The purple dye containing bromine was prepared by Phoenicians who lived in the city of _____.

A-B 12. Sodium and chlorine families form compounds by (A. sharing electrons; B. electrical attraction).

Water

Water is a well-known example of a compound formed by atoms that share electrons. Hydrogen has one electron and needs to gain another one to be like the inert gas helium. Oxygen needs two more electrons to be like neon. The water molecule, H_2O, has two hydrogen atoms and one oxygen atom. None of the atoms gain or lose electrons. Instead, they come together and share them.

Water is the most common liquid on earth. No other liqiud comes close. (Oil is probably second.) Despite being so common, the properties of water are extraordinary.

Pure water is odorless, colorless, and tasteless. It is an active chemical. Important substances of life such as starches, salts, and sugars can dissolve in water. Blood is about 80 percent water. It carries the chemicals of

ACTION

1. Many substances dissolved in water.

2. Water expanded as it froze, and ice floated on water.

3. Water resisted changes in temperature.

Can You Predict the Reactions?

life throughout the body. No other substance does as well. Chemists sometimes call water the universal solvent because so many substances will dissolve in it.

Chemists understand now why water is a solvent. Although it is electrically neutral overall, it does have regions with positive and negative electric charges.

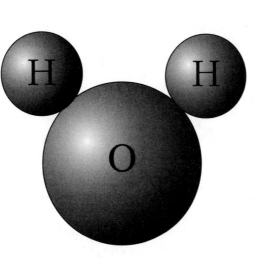

Water molecule

A diagram of a water molecule shows it with the shape like that of a cartoon face with big ears. The large oxygen atom is the face and the smaller hydrogen atoms are the ears. Although oxygen shares electrons with hydrogen, the oxygen atom holds them more tightly. The electric charge is not equally shared. In the neighborhood of the oxygen atom, the water molecule has a region with a negative charge. Around the hydrogen atoms the molecule has regions with a positive charge.

The charged regions give water the ability to dissolve different substances, especially salt. When salt crystals are shaken into water, the charged regions of the water molecule help it wiggle between sodium and chlorine, weakening their attraction and separating them. Salt crystals come apart and dissolve in water.

Water has another unusual property. Liquid water expands when it changes into ice. Most substances get smaller as they cool. As a red-hot bar of iron cools, it contracts. A bar of iron dropped into molten iron sinks to the bottom.

Water reverses this general rule. Solid water (ice) floats in water. This is important for living things, for if ice sank in water, the results would be disastrous. Suppose ice sank rather than floated. Imagine a lake in winter. As the surface cooled, ice would sink to the bottom. The warmer water that rose and replaced it would also cool and sink, too. In this way, the entire lake would cool to the freezing point. Slowly, the lake would freeze solid from bottom to top. The freezing water would kill any life in the lake.

In summer, water from melting ice would pool on top. The frozen bottom of the lake would be away from the sun's rays and stay frozen. Long before the lake thawed out, winter would begin again. As the years passed, even the largest lakes and the oceans would freeze solid. The entire world would be in the icy grip of a permanent deep freeze.

This does not happen. Instead, ice floats on water and that makes all the difference.

Again, imagine a lake in winter. This time, picture what actually does happen. As the water cools near freezing, it does not sink. Instead, it stays on the surface. Warm water remains on bottom. When ice forms, it floats on the surface.

Ice not only floats but also is a good insulator of heat. When a pond freezes, the layer of ice acts as a protective and insulating covering. It keeps the rest of the water from being exposed to cold air. The pond never freezes solid unless it is quite small. Fish and other water life are able to live through even the coldest winter.

Beavers in ponds in the far north have learned another trick of survival. After the pond behind their dam has a thick layer of ice, the beavers release some water. The water that drains away leaves an air gap under the ice. The ice and air gap is an effective way to keep out the cold. The small beaver pond stays liquid throughout a bitterly cold winter.

Snow is a better insulator than ice. It conducts heat poorly. Animals and plant life buried in a blanket of snow actually stay warmer than they would if the snow were not present. Many plants would be killed in harsh winters if they were not buried in a blanket of snow. Some animals survive blizzards by seeking refuge under a snowdrift. Outdoor hikers caught in blizzards build walls of snow to protect them from the howling wind. Snow does not provide heat. Instead, the numerous pockets of air in the snow prevent body heat from escaping.

During winter, almost one-fourth of the earth's land surface becomes covered with snow. Winter snow acts as a storehouse of fresh water. During spring, when plants and crops first begin growing, a steady and dependable supply of water is especially important. Usually the snow does not melt suddenly. Instead, the runoff from melting snow feeds rivers and supplies water for irrigation throughout most of the growing

Snow and ice act as an insulating barrier from cold temperatures.

season. The Bible mentions the storehouses of snow in Job 38:22. This may reference snow as a water reserve.

The Nile is an example of how snow can play a role in world history. Egypt was an important country during Bible times. Joseph and his family moved to Egypt to escape a terrible drought in their homeland. The Nile River watered Egypt. The Nile flowed through a desert for a thousand miles. Irrigation canals provided moisture for crops on either side. Vegetation grew in this 12-mile strip even during times of drought. Through the blazing summer, the river carried life-giving water because snow in the faraway mountains melted and fed into the Nile.

Why does water expand as it freezes? Why is ice lighter than water? Why is snow a good insulator? The first clue came from the shape of snowflakes. Snow is made of small crystals of frozen water. The crystals form directly as water vapor freezes around solid particles in the air. Snowflakes are alike in that all have an open, six-sided, hexagon shape. They are different because the patterns seem to be endless.

Wilson A. Bentley was the first person to call attention to the wonderful patterns in snowflakes. He was a farmer and amateur weather observer who lived in Jericho, Vermont.

As a teenager, Wilson Bentley received a microscope as a gift. He examined everything he could with it, including snowflakes. As he peered into the microscope, he tried to sketch their marvelous design. Many were so fragile they collapsed or melted before he finished the drawing. He made more than 300 sketches and saw that no two snowflakes were alike.

Snowflake crystals differ depending on the temperature and humidity. In very cold and dry conditions the flakes are tiny and made of pointed little crystals. In warmer

Melting snow from faraway mountains feeds water into the Nile.

and humid weather, they fall as much bigger and more intricate flakes. He wanted to capture all of the beautiful designs. Could he photograph a snow crystal?

He learned about a camera that could take pictures through a microscope. Its cost? One hundred dollars! In the 1880s, a farm worker would do well to earn one hundred dollars in a year. His family knew of his interest and saved the money for the camera. They presented it to him for his 17th birthday.

Wilson Bentley learned photography, including developing his own negatives. Photography through a microscope was especially difficult. Bentley worked in an unheated woodshed that was freezing cold. He did his best work when the temperature hovered around 0°F. For two years he had nothing good to show others. Finally, on January 15, 1885, Wilson A. Bentley, at age 19, became the first person to photograph a snow crystal.

In 1898 he visited Professor George Perkins at the University of Vermont. The professor recognized the scientific value of Bentley's pictures. Professor Perkins urged Bentley to publish articles describing his work.

Bentley sent articles to the United States Weather Service. They printed the articles in their technical magazine, the Monthly Weather Review. Wilson Bentley became one of the nation's best-known amateur weather observers. Hundreds of magazines published his photographs. The Encyclopedia Britannica and Webster's Dictionary both used his photographs to illustrate their articles on snowflakes. In 1924, the American Meteorological Society awarded Bentley a grant to prepare 2,500 of his best snow crystal pictures for publication. The book, *Snow Crystals*, earned respect from scientists and inspired wonder at creation in the minds of ordinary people.

Snowflakes remained Wilson Bentley's hobby. He became known as "Snowflake" Bentley. He made no money from his snow photographs. He always provided them at cost to interested scientists. He continued to earn his living as a farmer.

Bentley was a humble man, a Christian, who saw the Creator's hand in the intricate and beautiful snow crystals. In one of his articles, Bentley wrote, "Perhaps no natural

Wilson Bentley

and hail. Liquid water flows in rivers, lakes, and oceans. Water, as a gas, is invisible, but can be seen when it condenses to small droplets in clouds. Water changes into steam when the molecules of the water travel so fast they break away from the surface and go into the atmosphere. Water can change into a gas by evaporation or by boiling.

Evaporation takes place because not all water molecules travel at the same speed. During the random and ceaseless motion of molecules in water, they bump into one another. Some lose speed and energy during the collisions, but others gain speed and energy. Individual molecules with above average speed may have enough energy to escape from the surface and pass into the atmosphere.

The air can hold only so much water, so if the air is dry (low humidity) water will evaporate more quickly. If the air is humid, water does not evaporate as quickly. As the air above the water fills with water molecules, evaporation slows. Wind aids in evaporation because the wind carries away the air saturated with water vapor to replace it with fresh air of lower humidity.

Boiling is fast evaporation. If water is heated to 100°C (212°F), then most of the molecules have enough speed to escape. Boiling begins. Those molecules that escape carry away the most energy, so heat has to be continually applied for the boiling to continue.

Generally, the boiling temperature of liquid compounds made of atoms that share electrons depends on the atomic weight of the molecules. Those that are heavy are harder to get moving and do not boil as readily as lightweight molecules. Most substances with an atomic weight

phenomenon occurring upon the earth is more of an object lesson, or portrays more fully both the power and majesty, and the gentleness of the Creator, than does a wide-spread snowstorm."

Bentley's beautiful photographs did much to cause chemists to look at snow crystals. The six-sided hexagon patterns gave them a clue about the way that water molecules interact with one another. At room temperature, water molecules move around and bounce off one another with no particular pattern. As water cools, the molecules slow down and the unequal distribution of charge on the surface of the water molecules causes them to link up with one another. They take up an open hexagon pattern. This leaves a lot of empty space making ice lighter than liquid water. This explains why ice floats on water.

The three states of matter are solid, liquid, and gas. Solid water is ice, snow, sleet,

Solids, like ice, have slow- moving molecules.

Liquids, like water, have faster-moving molecules.

Gases, such as steam, have even faster-moving molecules.

similar to water become gases at far lower temperatures than water does. For instance, methane, CH_4, molecules weigh about the same as water molecules. Methane boils at -162°C (-259°F). That is 258 degrees below zero Fahrenheit! Water, on the other hand, boils at 100°C (212°F).

Why is this? Why does water remain a liquid at a higher temperature than methane? Methane is made of one carbon atom and four hydrogen atoms. Carbon, like water, holds electrons more tightly than hydrogen atoms. However, in the methane molecule, the four hydrogen atoms are arranged in an equal pattern all around the carbon atom. It forms a tetrahedron, a pyramid-like structure with the carbon atom in the middle and a hydrogen atom at each of the four corners. The methane molecule has no regions with an electric charge. Methane molecules do not attract one another very strongly. Without the attraction, they do not resist boiling. Methane evaporates and boils at a far lower temperature than water.

Water molecules, on the other hand, have negative and positive regions. They tend to be attracted to one another. Water molecules tend to stick together because of this electrical attraction. Water molecules resist flying away from each other. Water has to be heated to a higher temperature before the molecules will separate. No other common substance has the special properties of water.

Breaking the bonds holding water molecules to one another takes heat energy. Even a small amount of water can absorb a tremendous amount of heat. Water acts as a heat bank. It holds heat better than any other common substance. Water can hold 30 times as much heat as the same weight of lead.

Vast oceans cover much of the earth's surface. Ocean water absorbs heat in winter and releases it in summer, helping to moderate the earth's temperature.

Consider an island like Puerto Rico. The Caribbean Sea washes upon its southern shore and the Atlantic Ocean washes on the other. The temperature is pleasant the year around. On the other hand, the Sahara Desert is about the same distance from the equator as Puerto Rico. But it is far from any water. The Sahara suffers extreme temperatures. Days are blazing hot. Nights are chilly.

Without an atmosphere the moon's temperatures vary from 200°F on the sunlit side and -100°F on the dark side.

An extreme example is the earth's moon. The moon orbits the earth, so it is, on average, the same distance from the sun as the earth. The moon has no water. For that reason, temperatures jump to more than 93°C (200°F) on the sunlit side. After the sun sets, temperatures plunge to -73°C (-100°F).

Water's ability to resist changes in temperature helps living things. It regulates internal temperatures. Humans must keep their body temperatures constant or death will occur. It is risky for the human body to fall below 31°C (88°F) or rise above 41°C (105°F). Water keeps the body in this narrow temperature range. When the body becomes too hot, blood veins next to the skin enlarge. Blood flows closer to the surface and is cooled by the air. Perspiration from sweat glands and water vapor from the breath carry away excess heat.

So important is water that God chose it as a symbol of His love. The Bible calls Jesus the "Water of Life" (John 4:13–14). Jesus said, "If any man thirst, let him come unto me, and drink" (John 7:37).

Chemists understand water's importance to the physical world. As they examine its many unique properties,

they are struck by how it was perfectly designed for the needs of life on earth. Only a caring God could have designed water with these properties. As the Bible says in Psalm 33:5, "The earth is full of the goodness of the Lord."

Water and salt illustrate the two main ways that compounds form from atoms. Salt contains sodium and chlorine. The sodium gives up an electron and becomes positively charged. Chlorine accepts the electron and becomes negatively charged. The two charged atoms attract one another and form salt. On the other hand, neither oxygen nor hydrogen gives up electrons. Instead they share the ones they have.

REACTION

1. Molecules of other substances were attracted to the uneven electric charge around the water molecule.

2. Wilson Bentley's snowflake photographs were evidence that water molecules attract one another to make a light-weight open structure.

3. Water molecules absorbed heat because of the electrical attraction between molecules.

A-B   1.   Oxygen and hydrogen form the water molecule by (A. exchanging; B. sharing) electrons.

T F   2.   Water is the commonest liquid on earth.

A-D   3.   A diagram of a water molecule shows it as (A. a constantly shifting molecule that is never the same way twice; B. a long chain; C. an oxygen atom face with hydrogen atom ears; D. a molecule shaped like a pyramid).

A-B   4.   Liquid water (A. expands; B. contracts) when it changes into ice.

A-B   5.   Ice (A. floats; B. sinks) in water.

A-B   6.   Snow conducts heat (A. well; B. poorly).

A-D   7.   The Nile River continues to flow through deserts because (A. it is fed by desert springs; B. it is fed by melting snow in the mountains; C. rain falls year-round in Egypt; D. water is too heavy to evaporate).

A-D   8.   The first person to photograph a snowflake was (A. a French scientist; B. a Vermont teenager who lived on a farm; C. a Civil War photographer; D. a United States president who was an amateur scientist).

T F   9.   Wilson Bentley became wealthy from his hobby of photographing snowflakes.

A-B   10.   In cool water, molecules move more (A. quickly; B. slowly) than in warm water.

A-D   11.   Water boils at (A. 0°C [32°F]; B. 100°C [212°F]; C. -161°C [-258°F]; D. various temperatures depending on the phase of the moon).

A-B   12.   The one that boils at a hotter temperature is (A. methane; B. water).

A-D   13.   The main reason Puerto Rico has a milder climate than the Sahara Desert is that Puerto Rico (A. is an island surrounded by water; B. is closer to the equator; C. does not have a ready supply of sand; D. is nearer to the North Pole).

Carbon and Its Compounds

Carbon is an unusual element. The number of its compounds exceeds those made by all other elements by a wide margin. The other elements, more than 100, have about 50,000 compounds. Yet, carbon, only one element, has more than 3,000,000 (three million) compounds.

How does carbon form so many compounds?

Its need for electrons gives the answer. Carbon needs four more electrons to have its electrons in the stable arrangement like the electrons of neon. An atom of carbon readily shares electrons with a variety of elements to gain those electrons. It forms compounds with other carbon atoms and with hydrogen, oxygen, nitrogen, chlorine, fluorine, and many other elements.

Methane, CH_4, is one of the simplest carbon compounds. It was known as

ACTION

1. Carbon formed more compounds than all the other elements combined.

2. A tank that should have contained fluorine was empty.

3. Crude oil that seeped to the surface was a nuisance.

Can You Predict the Reactions?

marsh gas to the early chemists because it bubbled up from ponds filled with decaying plant matter. John Dalton was the English scientist who proposed the atomic theory of matter. He would take his students to a pond to collect marsh gas for study. A student filled a jar with water and held it upside down in the pool. John Dalton stirred the mud and released the methane. It bubbled to the surface and was collected in the jar.

Students asked questions about the gas. John Dalton grew interested in chemistry as he experimented with methane to answer their questions. He showed that methane was a colorless, odorless gas that burned with a blue flame. Later, chemists learned that a methane molecule has a single carbon atom sharing electrons with four hydrogen atoms. A hydrocarbon is any compound that contains only carbon and hydrogen. (Notice that the word hydrocarbon divides into "hydro" and "carbon," showing that it contains hydrogen and carbon.)

Chemists find it convenient to draw pictures to show carbon compounds. Structural formulas show the general shape of the molecule. A dash, —, represents two shared electrons. The structural formula for methane is:

$$\begin{array}{c} \text{H} \\ | \\ \text{H} - \text{C} - \text{H} \\ | \\ \text{H} \end{array}$$

Natural gas is a mixture of methane and a similar hydrocarbon known as ethane, C_2H_6. Methane collects in coal mines where it is an explosive danger. Natural gas also forms over oil deposits in the ground. For decades, it was considered

Natural gas is used in heating and cooking and as a fuel in industry.

a nuisance. Oil wells released the gas and it was burned as it escaped to prevent an explosion. At the time, there was no particular use for the gas. Later, chemists showed that it could be used as a fuel. When burned with oxygen, natural gas releases carbon dioxide and water. It burns cleaner than coal or wood. Unlike solid fuels such as coal or wood, natural gas can flow through cross-country pipelines.

Today pipes carry natural gas into the home for use in heating and cooking. It also serves as a fuel in industry and as a raw material for making plastics. Some cars have been converted so they will burn natural gas. The one danger from natural gas is that it is odorless. A leak would not normally be detected. Should the leaking gas build up in a home, a spark would cause a disastrous explosion. Gas companies add a sulfur compound to natural gas used in the home. The sulfur compound has a noticeable odor. A gas leak is immediately obvious to any nearby nose.

Other elements can replace one or more of the hydrogen atoms in methane. This gives an entirely new carbon compound. Three chlorine atoms can replace three hydrogen atoms. The result is chloroform, $CHCl_3$.

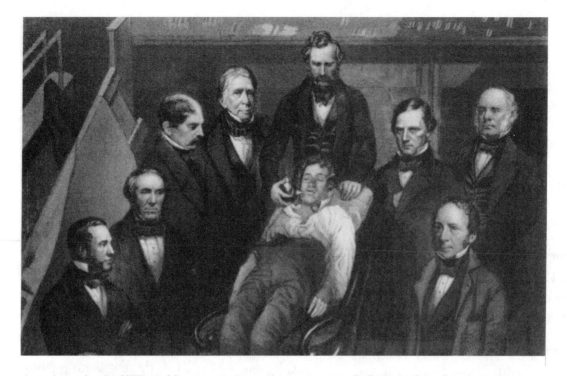

American dentist William Morton used a carbon compound, diethyl ether, for the purpose of putting people to sleep and deadening pain.

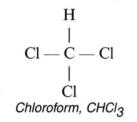

Chloroform, CHCl₃

Chloroform, $CHCl_3$, contains one carbon atom, one hydrogen atom, and three chlorine atoms. It is a clear, colorless liquid with a sweet odor. It can put people to sleep and deaden pain. In 1847, James Simpson, a Scottish physician, used it to put people to sleep during surgery. A year earlier, the American dentist William Morton had used another carbon compound, diethyl ether, $C_2H_5OC_2H_5$, for the same purpose. Chloroform and ether were the first compounds used to render a patient insensitive to pain during surgery.

Chloroform had to be stored properly. If light struck it, chloroform changed into deadly phosgene gas $COCl_2$. It also had to be given to the patient in carefully measured doses. Too little and the patient felt the pain; too much and the patient never woke up. Other anesthetics have replaced chloroform for most surgical operations. However, it is still used in primitive conditions because it does not explode when exposed to open flame and it remains a liquid in hot climates.

If all four of the hydrogen atoms of methane are replaced with chlorine, the result is carbon tetrachloride, CCl_4. The name comes from carbon, tetra meaning four, and chloride from chlorine. Carbon tetrachloride contains one carbon atom and four chlorine atoms.

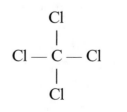

Carbon tetrachloride, CCl₄

Chloroform and carbon tetrachloride differ only by one atom, yet this small change makes all the difference in the properties of the two compounds. As a vapor, carbon tetrachloride is heavier than air. It does not burn. Some fire extinguishers use carbon tetrachloride. When pumped over a fire as a liquid, it immediately changes to a heavy blanket of suffocating vapor and smothers the flame. Carbon tetrachloride easily dissolves organic compounds such as fats, oils, and greases. Some fabrics shrink when exposed to water. They are dry cleaned with carbon tetrachloride. Carbon tetrachloride is a liquid but it is called a dry cleaner because it contains no water.

Like hydrogen, fluorine and chlorine need one more electron to have their electrons in a stable arrangement. They receive the extra electron by sharing it with carbon. Compounds of carbon, fluorine, or chlorine are especially stable. If a compound contains chlorine, fluorine, and carbon, it is known as chlorofluorocarbon, abbreviated CFC. The name is a combination of the words chlorine, fluorine, and carbon: chloro-fluoro-carbon. CFCs had a huge variety of uses from insulators in high voltage transformers to propellants in spray cans. However, scientists began to be concerned that they damaged the ozone layer.

The ozone layer is a gas in the upper atmosphere of the earth. Ozone is composed of three oxygen atoms combined into one molecule, O_3. The ozone layer intercepts harmful ultraviolet rays from

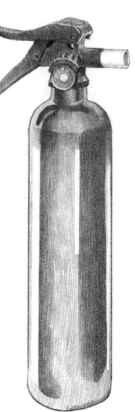

Some fire extinguishers use carbon tetrachloride.

the sun and filters them out before they strike the earth. Overexposure to ultraviolet rays are known to cause skin cancer. Chemists were concerned that a reduced ozone layer might result in an increase in cancer. They suggested that other compounds be used wherever possible rather than CFCs. Today, carbon dioxide, nitrogen, or ordinary air under pressure are used in spray cans.

Freon is an important chlorofluorocarbon compound used in refrigeration. Use of Freon is regulated to prevent its spread into the atmosphere. The simplest Freon molecule looks like the methane molecule but with fluorine and chlorine substituted for the four hydrogen atoms.

$$\begin{array}{c} Cl \\ | \\ F - C - F \\ | \\ Cl \end{array}$$

Freon, CCl_2F_2

Refrigerators and air conditioners use Freon. How does Freon cool? Perhaps, you have noticed that alcohol cools the skin due to its rapid evaporation. Whenever a liquid evaporates, it cools its surroundings. Freon cools when it changes from a liquid to a gas, too. Freon is normally a gas at room temperature. Putting it under pressure changes it into a liquid. A motor pumps liquid Freon under pressure to coils inside the refrigerator. A nozzle releases the pressure. Freon evaporates back into a gas and grows

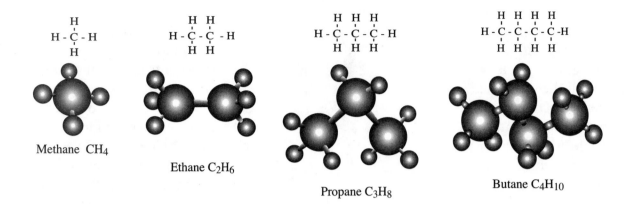

Methane CH$_4$

Ethane C$_2$H$_6$

Propane C$_3$H$_8$

Butane C$_4$H$_{10}$

cooler. Then the motor pumps it to the coils behind the refrigerator. There the motor pressurizes it again and changes it back into a liquid. The Freon releases heat to the air.

A refrigerator is a heat pump. It removes the heat from inside the refrigerator and releases it into the air outside the refrigerator.

Another way to make new carbon compounds from methane is to substitute the hydroxyl group, OH, for hydrogen. Hydroxyl is a combination of oxygen and hydrogen that stays together in some reactions. All alcohols contain the OH pair. When OH replaces hydrogen in methane, it forms an entirely new compound. It is methanol, CH$_3$OH, also known as methyl alcohol.

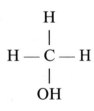

Methanol, CH$_3$OH
(methyl alcohol)

Methanol is a colorless liquid with a pleasant odor. It is also called wood alcohol. Methanol is a by-product of changing wood to charcoal. Wood heated without oxygen gives off vapors. Chemists condense the vapor to give methanol. Methanol is a good fuel. It burns with a hot, smokeless flame. Methanol is burned as a fuel in racing engines.

Methanol is poisonous. Drinking it or inhaling the vapors is extremely dangerous. A tablespoon of methanol can cause blindness and an ounce of it can cause death. Methanol can be absorbed into the bloodstream through the skin. Mechanics who work on cars that burn methanol have to be specially trained.

Smaller molecules can be combined to give new carbon compounds. Chemists can build a long series of hydrocarbon chains by adding to the methane molecule. Adding CH$_2$ to methane gives ethane. Adding CH$_2$ to ethane gives propane, and so on endlessly.

The fact that carbon can form long chains with itself is one reason that it can form so many compounds.

A hydrocarbon chain has carbon atoms joined with one another as the backbone of the compound. Hydrogen atoms attach themselves to the carbon atom at various locations. Hydrocarbons are the main molecules that make natural gas, petroleum, and lubricants. As the chains get longer, the compounds become more dense and heavy. The first few are gases such as methane, then they become liquids such as octane in automobile fuels, and finally they become solids such as paraffin in candles.

Hydrocarbons can be changed by replacing any of the hydrogen atoms with atoms of other elements. Hydrocarbons serve as the starting material for plastic, synthetic fibers, and artificial rubber.

Teflon is like a long hydrocarbon chain, but with fluorine attached to the carbon atoms instead of hydrogen. In the structural formula, the dots (. . .) show that the pattern continues to repeat. Teflon is a polymer and can be hundreds or even thousands of carbon atoms long. A molecule made from the same units strung together is a polymer. The word polymer is from poly meaning "many" and mer meaning "part." A polymer is made of many parts.

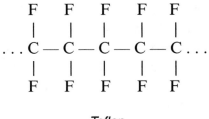

Teflon

Teflon was discovered in 1938. Roy J. Plunkett was a young chemist who worked for the Du Pont Company. He investigated gases such as Freon that might work for refrigeration. Because of its great activity, fluorine was stored by reacting it with carbon. The result was a gas that he kept in a tank. One morning he put a tank in place and opened the valve to send the gas containing fluorine through his test apparatus. No gas came out. What had happened to it?

He weighed the tank. It still weighed the same. The gas had not escaped. He cut off the valve and upended the tank. A few white flakes fell out. All of the gas had changed into a waxy, white substance. Tests showed that it did not conduct electricity, had a very slippery surface, and resisted the action of almost all chemicals including acids. It was inert.

Because it is so inert, other chemicals ignore it. Teflon is often used to coat medical implants in the human body. For example, pacemakers help the heart beat a steady rhythm. Pacemakers are coated with Teflon because the human body tolerates Teflon and does not try to reject it.

Teflon has many other uses. It gives a slippery surface to bearings for wheels and coats fishing line so it will not snag. Teflon does not melt until 320°C (608°F), which is hotter than most ovens. It is a good choice for nonstick frying pans. It also remains flexible in cold temperature. Space suits are coated in Teflon. (The first letter of both Teflon and Freon are capital to show that they are registered trademarks of the Du Pont Company.)

Some people call Teflon an accidental discovery. However, another chemist may have been irritated that the gas for his experiment had changed form. Instead of dismissing the white flakes as a bother, Roy Plunkett tested the new compound and found important uses for it. The American inventor Thomas Edison said, "Chance favors the prepared mind." Roy Plunkett was wise enough to recognize good fortune and not dismiss it.

Two of the carbon compounds that early chemists investigated were ethyl alcohol and dimethyl ether. To their surprise, they found that the two compounds had the same chemical formula: C_2H_6O. Yet, despite containing the same atoms in the same numbers, their properties were far different.

Pure ethyl alcohol is a clear, colorless

liquid with a burning taste. It is known as ethanol or grain alcohol. It can be made from grains such as corn or from plants that contains starch such as potatoes. In the United States and elsewhere, ethanol is blended with gasoline and burned as a fuel in automobiles. Ethyl alcohol is also the main ingredient in intoxicating beverages. Because the drinking variety is heavily taxed, the alcohol for other purposes has a foul-tasting substance added so it cannot be consumed.

Dimethyl ether contains the same atoms in the same numbers as ethyl alcohol. However, dimethyl ether is a gas at room temperature. The two compounds are very different in their properties. The difference lies in the arrangement of the atoms.

Ethyl alcohol and dimethyl ether are examples of isomers. Isomers have exactly the same type and number of atoms, but different shapes. The word isomer is made of iso meaning "the same" and mer meaning "parts." Isomers contain the same parts.

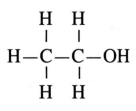

Ethyl alcohol

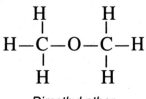

Dimethyl ether

Hydrocarbon chains are world champions at forming isomers. For instance, every butane molecule has four carbon atoms. The atoms can be put together in two ways. In one molecule, the atoms are in a straight line. The other one has a side branch. Although they have the same chemical formula C_4H_{10}, the two butane molecules do differ slightly. The one with the side chain burns less vigorously than normal butane. It is more difficult to change into a liquid.

As the number of carbon atoms increase, the number of possible isomers increase, too. As the chains grow longer, side branches can form. Even side branches can themselves have side chains. For example, a hydrocarbon chain with 10 carbon atoms can be put together in 75 different ways.

To make carbon compounds, chemists begin with natural sources of hydrocarbons. The most common supply of the hydrocarbons is in crude oil, or petroleum. The word petroleum is from the Latin words *petra* meaning "rock" and *oleum* meaning "oil." Petroleum is rock oil. Petroleum is the second-most common liquid on earth. Water is first.

Crude oil is a dark, thick fluid found underground in many parts of the world. Usually crude oil stays below the ground. Sometimes, pressure sends it to the surface. Sunlight turns it into pitch, a sticky tar-like substance.

The Bible describes how Pharaoh in Egypt ordered the slaughter of newborn Hebrew boys. The mother of baby Moses made an ark of bulrushes, a reed-like plant. She smeared the ark with slime and with pitch. She laid him inside the ark of bulrushes and hid him along the Nile River. The pitch described in Exodus 2:3 could be tar from crude oil.

Until the middle of the 1800s, crude

Ancient people applied pitch to seal and waterproof structures and sailing vessels.

oil had few useful purposes. Ambitious salesmen bottled the foul-smelling stuff and sold it as a medicine. It tasted so awful it had to be good!

Lamps of that day burned oil made from the fat of whales. In 1847, James Young, a Scotsman, made oil for lamps from coal. He called it coal oil. In the United States, Abraham Gessner heated shale, a type of rock that contains oil. The heat drove out the oil. Gessner called his product kerosene. Lamps could burn either coal oil or kerosene in place of whale oil.

In the late 1850s, chemists learned how to make kerosene from crude oil.

Kerosene from petroleum cost less than whale oil. It soon became the preferred oil for lamps. This set off a search for crude oil. Until then, folks kept away from land with oil on the surface. The black slime turned the water bad and killed crops. Suddenly, the same land became valuable.

Edwin L. Drake, a retired railroad conductor, believed he could pump oil from below the ground. Two lawyers with money to invest backed his efforts. Drake began drilling in June 1859, near the small town of Titusville in western Pennsylvania. People made fun of him.

They called the project "Drake's folly."

On August 27, 1859, Drake struck oil at a depth of 69.5 feet. Drake's folly soon pumped 25 barrels of crude oil a day. Edwin L. Drake drilled the first successful oil well in the United States.

Kerosene remained the main product of oil until the invention of the automobile. Internal combustion engines ran on gasoline, so it came into great demand. Ever since that time, the value of crude oil has grown. People called it black gold.

One hundred gallons of crude oil give about 50 gallons of gasoline. Oil companies don't waste the other 50 gallons. They turn it into many useful products. Heating oil, lubricating oils, and greases are made from the heavier and longer hydrocarbon chains in petroleum. Petroleum jelly, better known by the brand name of Vaseline, is even thicker than grease. It is an odorless and tasteless jelly-like substance. It is rubbed on dry skin and chapped lips.

Paraffin wax is heavier still. The hydrocarbon chains in it are longer than the hydrocarbon chains in petroleum jelly. Paraffin is a milky-white solid, oily to the touch. Candles are made of paraffin. A cotton wick is surrounded by paraffin. When the wick is lighted, the paraffin burns, producing heat and light. Coating cardboard cartons with paraffin makes them waterproof. One of Thomas A. Edison's many inventions was paper coated with paraffin. He invented waxed paper. The wax is paraffin.

Asphalt is what remains when chemists remove everything else from crude oil. Its main use is as a paving material and waterproof sealer. Sometimes asphalt forms naturally. When pitch bakes in the sun, it changes into asphalt. One of the largest natural deposits of asphalt is on the island of Trinidad in the Caribbean. An asphalt lake there covers 115 acres and is at least 285 feet deep.

Petroleum is conveniently located for use by mankind. This is one evidence for the providence of God — God will provide. If it were deeper, recovering the oil would be nearly impossible. If it were located less deeply than it is, and found its way to the surface, it would turn to hard asphalt. The Bible says that the earth is the Lord's (Psalms 24:1) and that God created all things (Ephesians 3:9). God is a loving Father. He provides us with the oil we need for cooking, heating, motor fuel, and other everyday products.

REACTION

1. Carbon atoms shared electrons with other elements in many different ways.

2. Roy J. Plunkett discovered that fluorine and carbon gas had changed into solid Teflon.

3. Kerosene from crude oil replaced whale oil in lamps.

1. Carbon needs _____ more electrons to have its electrons in the stable arrangement like the electrons of neon.

A-D 2. Methane is also known as (A. marsh; B. mustard; C. poison; D. tear) gas.

A-D 3. A hydrocarbon is a compound that contains only carbon and (A. chlorine; B. fluorine; C. hydrogen; D. oxygen).

A-B 4. When burned with oxygen, natural gas releases carbon dioxide and (A. sulfuric acid; B. water).

T F 5. A sulfur compound is added to natural gas so a leak can be detected by the smell.

A-D 6. The one that has been used to put people to sleep during operations is (A. carbon tetrachloride; B. chloroform; C. oxygen; D. salt).

7. The number of chlorine atoms in carbon tetrachloride is _____.

T F 8. Carbon tetrachloride is used for dry cleaning because it is a dry powder.

T F 9. The ozone layer reduces the effect of harmful ultraviolet rays from the sun.

T F 10. Freon is used for refrigeration.

T F 11. Whenever a liquid evaporates, it warms its surroundings.

T F 12. Methanol is burned as a fuel in racing engines.

A-B 13. Paraffin is an example of a (A. short; B. long) hydrocarbon chain.

A-D 14. Teflon is an example of (A. an isobar; B. an isomer; C. a pachyderm; D. a polymer.

A-B 15. Teflon is (A. sticky; B. slick).

A-C 16. Ethyl alcohol and dimethyl ether have the same (A. chemical formula; B. properties; C. structures).

A-B 17. Ethyl alcohol and dimethyl ether are examples of (A. polymers; B. isomers).

A-D 18. Petroleum means (A. floor covering; B. pet rock; C. rock oil; D. written on stone.

Organic Chemistry

Have you ever played the game 20 questions? One person thinks of an item and the contestant tries to figure out what it is by asking questions. The limit is 20 questions. The first question is usually, "Is it vegetable, animal, or mineral?" Early chemists asked a similar question when they discovered a new compound. Was it from the natural nonliving environment or did it come from plants or animals?

Almost all the ancient substances — metals, minerals, acids, bases, salts, gases in the air — occurred naturally in the earth, oceans, and air. They were not alive and never had been alive. They were part of the nonliving environment. Nonliving compounds such as sand, rock crystals, and other minerals would not burn. A chemist could heat salt until it became red hot. Once cooled, it was still salt.

ACTION

1. Organic compounds were difficult to make in the laboratory.

2. Chemists could not describe the structure of benzene, a simple carbon compound.

3. Dyes and perfumes came from plants and animals.

4. Carbolic acid reacted with formaldehyde to make a solid that resisted the action of water and alcohol.

Can You Predict the Reactions?

The other compounds were those that came from living organisms. They included sugar, starch, glue, gelatin, silk, rubber, cellulose, and foods. Living plants and animals manufactured these substances. For instance, sugar came from sugar cane, sugar beets, or sugar maple trees. Most organic compounds would burn. Wood, fat, and oil burned and could be used as fuels. Unlike nonliving compounds, those from plants or animals could not resist heat. When a chemist heated sugar, it turned black. Once cooled it was no longer sugar. It broke down into carbon and water.

Chemists gave the name "organic" to substances from living things. Organic means "from the organs." Organic substances come from plants or animals, but not from nonliving matter. Organic compounds have complex chemical formulas. Sugar is one of the simplest organic molecules. Table sugar, $C_{12}H_{22}O_{11}$, has 45 atoms: 12 carbon atoms, 22 hydrogen atoms and 11 oxygen atoms.

Plants are organic substances.

Although organic compounds contained a large number of atoms, the number of different atoms was small. Organic compounds always contained carbon, C, along with a few other elements. Usually present were hydrogen, oxygen, and nitrogen.

Chemists could make inorganic compounds such as water by burning oxygen gas and hydrogen gas. Salt could easily be made by combining sodium and chlorine. But organic compounds resisted all efforts to make them in the laboratory. Countless experiments failed to form even the simplest sugar molecule. Chemists could not coach carbon, hydrogen, and oxygen atoms together to give sugar.

After years of trying, chemists decided that chemical laws did not apply to organic compounds. Instead, they proposed that organic compounds could arise only through a vital force within a living cell. According to this view, only living tissue could make an organic compound. The only way to make sugar was to extract it from sugar cane, sugar beets, or sugar maple trees. Making it in the laboratory from raw materials was impossible, the chemists said.

In 1845, Hermann Kolbe, a German chemist, produced acetic acid, CH_3COOH, from raw materials. Acetic acid gives vinegar its sour taste. Vinegar, in turn, is produced from the juice of grapes. Chemists agreed that it was an organic substance. Kolbe began with hydrogen, carbon, and oxygen atoms and combined them to give acetic acid.

Kolbe showed that chemicals can react in the nonliving environment, inside living tissue, or in the laboratory. Regardless of where they occur, chemical reactions follow the same set of chemical laws. Later, Hermann Kolbe made salicylic acid, a complicated organic substance. It is found in some fruits and a derivative of it makes the active ingredient in asprin.

Organic chemistry came into its own as a separate field of study. What about the term organic? Chemists could make organic compounds outside the organs of living bodies. Should the name be dropped? The question came up at the gathering of chemists at the famous International Chemical Congress, which met in Karlsruhe, Germany, in 1860.

August Kekulé, a German chemist, attended the conference. He thought about the problem and a year later offered a solution. He noticed that all organic compounds contained carbon. His idea was to reserve the name organic for carbon compounds. Chemists agreed to this change.

Organic chemistry is the study of carbon compounds. Today, organic chemistry, the chemistry of carbon compounds, plays an important role in our daily lives. Food, vitamins, drugs, medicines, fuels, dyes, perfumes, flavors, detergents, plastics, rubber, and fibers are all organic compounds.

Chemists of the 1800s worked out the structural formulas of many carbon compounds. But the structure of benzene, a toxic liquid, remained a mystery. It was a simple compound with only 12 atoms, six carbon atoms and six hydrogen atoms, C_6H_6. It is a hydrocarbon because it contains hydrogen and carbon. Benzene was made from coal tar. Chemists used it as an ingredient in dyes and explosives. Because of its many important uses, chemists needed to understand benzene's structure.

August Kekulé

August Kekulé attacked the problem of benzene. It should have been simple. After all, how many different ways can one put together six carbon atoms and six hydrogen atoms? His designs fell short of agreeing with the experimental evidence. He put the problem aside. Then, in a flash of brilliance the answer came to Kekulé as he napped on a horsedrawn vehicle with other passengers. The six carbon atoms he had been drawing while awake took on a life of their own in his troubled dreams. They became six little monkey-like figures leering at him because of his inability to make sense of benzene. Then the monkeys began whirling around one another. One monkey grabbed the tail of the other. Soon the six animals formed a spinning ring. Instead of a chain, benzene was a hydrocarbon ring!

Kekulé announced his finding in 1865. Chemists soon proved his design to be the correct structure of benzene. With the structural formula of benzene before them, chemists could build other compounds. They made dyes, drugs, paints, solvents, scents, perfumes, adhesives, and plastics from benzene. About half of all carbon compounds have the chain-like form of hydrocarbons. The other half has the circular form of benzene.

Starting in the 1850s, chemists began pursuing synthetic compounds in earnest. A synthetic compound is one made in the laboratory by combining elements or groups of elements. A teenage boy invented the first successful synthetic product. His name was William Henry Perkin.

Perkin's father wanted him to become an architect. The young student persuaded his father to let him study chemistry at the Royal College in London.

During the middle of the 1800s, chemistry in England had reached a low point. Most schools did not even teach chemistry. Queen Victoria realized that her country was behind others in chemical research. She invited the well-known German chemist August Hofmann to teach chemistry in England.

William Henry Perkin was fortunate to be able to study in Hofmann's classes. Professor Hofmann delivered his lectures with drama and flair. Assistants performed experiments as he spoke. The very reactions that Hofmann described took place before the students' eyes.

One day Hofmann wondered whether someone could make quinine in the laboratory. Quinine fought malaria, a tropical disease. Chemists extracted it from the bark of a South American tree. A supply of quinine would be a real advantage to England. British citizens lived in many tropical regions where malaria was common. A synthetic supply of quinine would keep the British from being at the mercy of those who supplied the natural variety.

During Easter vacation of 1856, Perkin gave himself the ambitious task of making quinine in his home laboratory.

William Perkin

Chemists now know that he simply could not have succeeded. Neither he nor any other chemist knew quinine's structure. Quinine is a complex molecule. Chemists of the 1850s had neither the knowledge nor the laboratory skill to put together big molecules. The feat of making quinine wasn't accomplished until 1944 by the American chemist Robert Woodward. Perkin's quest for quinine was doomed to failure. He didn't know this, so he experimented anyway. He tried several approaches. He experimented with aniline, a benzene compound that contains nitrogen. The reaction created a gummy mess. As he started to clean away the products of the reaction, a purple glint caught his eye. Perkin mixed alcohol to extract the colored substance. The alcohol turned an intense purple.

Perkin wondered if his discovery would make a satisfactory dye. Textile makers use dyes to color fabrics. A satisfactory dye attaches itself firmly to the fabric. It resists fading caused by exposure to sunlight, stains, or perspiration. It does not bleach out when washed.

The young chemistry student sent a sample of his discovery to a textile company in Scotland. He asked if it might serve to color fabric. The substance proved to be a very effective coloring agent. Owners of the fabric factory offered to buy it provided Perkin could supply it cheaply and in large amounts.

William Henry Perkin called his dye aniline purple. He investigated to see if

England would grant a patent to a teenager. The answer was yes, so he took out a patent on the process.

Making a substance in test tubes in a laboratory is vastly simpler than making it in commercial quantities. Perkin, his father, and a brother set out to make the dye. Practically none of the equipment they needed was available. They had to make it themselves. In addition, raw materials for the process were not available in England. Aniline was a rare substance, found in only a few research laboratories. Perkin had to buy benzene and make aniline from it. For this, he needed strong nitric acid, which he manufactured, too.

Until Perkin's discovery, dyes came from plants and animals. Within a few years, dyes were synthetic. Even the royal color indigo was synthesized. Indigo plantations in the Far East suffered economic ruin. Another synthetic dye replaced alizarin, a natural red dye from the madder plant. Almost from one season to the next, the demand for madder plants plummeted. Farmers who didn't switch to other crops went broke.

For almost 20 years, Perkin devoted his time to making his dye factory a success. Perkin became England's best-known chemist. He became an extremely wealthy person. In 1874 he sold his holdings. He retired from industry and returned to chemical research.

Success struck a second time. Perkin developed the first synthetic perfume. He managed to synthesize coumarin, a fragrant compound extracted from plants. It has the pleasant odor of new-mown hay. His discovery opened the door to the synthetic perfume industry. He became a millionaire all over again.

Chemists researched ways to make synthetic copies of existing compounds. Starting near the 1800s, chemists discovered new compounds that had never existed before. A discovery by Leo Baekeland showed the way to a whole realm of compounds unlike any that existed in nature.

Leo Baekeland was a Belgian who traveled to the United States to study chemistry. He stayed in the United States and earned a living as a photographer. Photography was a chemical process that used silver compounds. Once exposed in the camera, the film could not be exposed to light or the image would be ruined. Making prints from the negative also had to be done in total darkness.

In 1891, Leo invented a photographic paper that could be developed under artificial light. George Eastman had founded the Eastman Kodak Company. Mr. Eastman paid one million dollars for rights to Leo's photographic paper.

Leo Baekeland invested the money in his chemical researches. He built a private research laboratory. He searched for a substitute for shellac, a type of sealing wax. Shellac was an organic compound

Perkin developed synthetic perfumes.

Telephones are one of the many products made from Bakelite.

produced by a tiny insect, the lac. Shellac could be dissolved in alcohol and the mixture painted on wood. Once dried, shellac gave wood a glossy finish and protected the wood from water and spills.

Leo wanted to make a substitute for shellac. Chemists warned him against heating carbolic acid, C_6H_5OH, with formaldehyde, HCHO. When the mixture cooled, it hardened solid. It resisted being dissolved by water, alcohol, or any other solvent. Chemists avoided even experimenting with those two substances. After the reaction, test tubes were so clogged they had to be tossed out.

Leo Baekeland experimented anyway. A substance that could resist water when it dried might make good shellac. He mixed carbolic acid and formaldehyde in a test tube. As expected, it hardened and plugged the test tube. He tried to find a way to dissolve the compound. If he could dissolve it, then it could be spread on wood like shellac. It would not soften when heated. It would not dissolve when treated with other

chemicals. How could he soften it to spread it on wood? Nothing worked. Leo had to discard a lot of laboratory glassware.

Finally, Leo realized he'd found something much more useful than shellac. A substance that resisted alcohol, acid, and water would be a useful material. He repeated the experiments with the goal of making the material even more durable. He produced a material quite unlike any other.

He named it Bakelite, a play on his name, the fact that it was light in weight and that it could withstand the heat of an oven. Bakelite was the first modern plastic. It was synthetic. A synthetic material is one made in the laboratory. Until then synthetic materials were based on those found in nature. His plastic was not only synthetic, it did not exist anywhere in nature.

Bakelite became very successful indeed. Although hard, it could be machined or cast into shape. It could be colored and dyed. For half a century, telephone receivers were made of black Bakelite. It is still used today. Because it is an electrical insulator, it is used for light switches. Because it can resist heat, it serves as pot handles. Automobile manufacturers use it for knobs and switches because it withstands heat, strong sunlight, and weathering.

Chemists soon produced other plastics with a variety of desirable properties. Some plastics were pound-for-pound stronger than steel. Today, plastic has become as important a building material as wood, stone, and steel. The United States produces more plastic than steel.

The word plastic means "capable of being shaped or formed." Plastics can be given almost any shape when they are first produced. After they cool, they retain the shape they were given. The range of their properties is nearly limitless. Clothing and jackets are made of plastic fibers that are as soft and warm as natural fibers. Plastics have a vast range in hardness. Some can be carved like wood while others resist the impact of a high-speed bullet.

Wings covered in lightweight plastic made it possible for a human pilot to power the Gossamer Condor. On August 23, 1977, this lightweight airplane completed a figure eight around two flagpoles one-half mile apart. The plane was designed by Dr. Paul MacCready Jr. and flown by Bryan Allen. The course was at the Shafter Airport in California. It won a prize offered by the Royal Aeronautical Society, London, England, for the first human-powered flight over a set course. Later, another plane, the Gossamer Albatross, became the first human-powered craft to cross the English Channel.

The Gossamer Albatross

Today, scientists are experimenting with high-flying radio-controlled aircraft so lightweight they can be powered by solar energy. The airplanes are designed to stay aloft for a month or more for environmental studies. Plastics make it possible.

Aniline purple and Bakelite are but two examples of the millions of carbon compounds. As the years passed, the number of carbon compounds continued to grow. Perkin and chemists of his day knew of about 12,000 carbon compounds. Baekeland and the chemists of the early 1900s knew of about 150,000. By 1940 chemists had cataloged 500,000 carbon compounds. In the 2000s, the number topped 3,000,000. Today, it grows by 100,000 or so each year.

More chemists earn a living working with carbon and its compounds than with all of the other elements combined.

R E A C T I O N

1. Herman Kolbe produced the organic compound acetic acid from raw materials.

2. August Kekulé found the structure of benzene to be a ring.

3. William Henry Perkin made the first synthetic dyes and perfumes.

4. Leo Baekeland made the first plastic.

A-B   1.   Salt is an example of a compound that is (A. formed by living organisms; B. found in the nonliving environment).

A-B   2.   Sugar is an example of a compound that is (A. formed by living organisms; B. found in the nonliving environment).

3.   The elements found in organic compounds include hydrogen, oxygen, nitrogen, and _____.

T F   4.   Chemical reactions follow a different set of rules in living things than they do in the laboratory.

T F   5.   No one has ever succeeded in making organic compounds in the laboratory.

A-D   6.   Today, organic chemistry is the chemistry of (A. carbon; B. hydrogen; C. nitrogen; D. oxygen) compounds.

7.   Benzene is a hydrocarbon (A. chain; B. ring).

A-D   8.   The one that fights malaria is (A. aniline purple; B. Bakelite; C. benzene; D. quinine).

A-D   9.   While trying to make quinine, William Henry Perkin discovered (A. a new plastic; B. a perfume substitute; C. a synthetic dye; D. a treatment for malaria).

T F   10.   Because he was a teenager, William Henry Perkin's father had to take out the patent on aniline purple.

T F   11.   After he became successful, William Henry Perkin retired from chemical research.

A-D   12.   Leo Baekeland discovered the substance he called Bakelite while trying to make a substitute for (A. a dye; B. a perfume; C. eye shadow; D. shellac).

A-D   13.   When Leo Baekeland mixed carbolic acid and formaldehyde, the result was (A. a substance that clogged test tubes; B. a substance with the smell of new-mown hay; C. a thin liquid; D. an explosive gas).

T F   14.   Although Bakelite was the first plastic, it was immediately replaced by better ones and proved a disappointing failure to Leo Baekeland.

A-D   15.   The word plastic means (A. capable of being shaped; B. cheap; C. phony; D. soft).

Chapter Thirteen

Nitrogen and Its Compounds

Like most dyes and drugs, explosives usually contain carbon. For that reason, chemists call them organic compounds. However, the essential element of explosives is not carbon but nitrogen.

Nitrogen is the gas that makes up four-fifths of the atmosphere. It is a colorless gas, and one without taste or smell. Nitrogen does not readily form compounds. Chemists must force it close to other atoms to share its electrons. This takes a lot of energy. Even so, the nitrogen bond is unstable. It easily breaks. The atoms fly apart with the energy that forced them together to make the nitrogen compound.

The Chinese are believed to have been the first to make explosive black powder. They combined charcoal (carbon), sulfur, and saltpeter (potassium nitrate). It came to Europe by way of the Arab world. The

ACTION

1. Nitrogen compounds were unstable and broke apart easily.

2. Liquid nitroglycerine was very dangerous to use.

3. Alfred Nobel was called a merchant of death because his explosive was used in military weapons.

Can You Predict the Reactions?

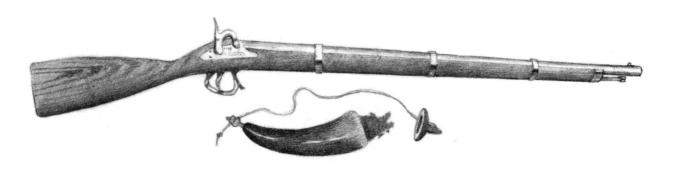

Musket and powder horn

Arabs fired projectiles from a hollow bamboo pole held together by iron bands. Rather than shooting a bullet, a charge of black powder shot an arrow. Europeans learned the secret of its manufacture in the 1200s. Black powder remained the only known explosive for six hundred years.

Black powder became known as gunpowder for use in early firearms. The powder was set off with the spark from flint, a type of stone. In addition to the hot sparks from flint, static electricity can cause it to explode. People who manufactured gunpowder took special care for safety. They crushed charcoal and sulfur into fine particles first, and then mixed them together. They kept the saltpeter separate until the last step.

The saltpeter in gunpowder tended to absorb moisture that caused guns to misfire. In frontier times, hunters kept the gunpowder in a sealed space in the side of the chimney. The advice to "keep your powder dry" is a reminder of this practice.

When gunpowder exploded, it generated carbon dioxide gas and nitrogen gas. Both were very hot. The rapid expansion of hot gases caused the destruction of an explosion. Gunpowder also released a lot of smoke. Only about 40 percent of gunpowder went into making the hot gases. The rest produced choking gas, smoke, and residue that fouled rifle barrels.

Miners objected to the smoke. When they used it to mine for coal, the explosion sent a rolling blast of choking gas along the mineshaft. They could not see until the smoke settled.

Soldiers liked the smoke even less. Soldiers could not fire on the enemy without revealing their positions. After firing their guns, a thick cloud of white smoke drifted up. The cloud showed the enemy the source of the shots. When cannons and guns fired at once, the smoke often obscured the battlefield. After every shot, soldiers had to swab the unburned residue from the gun and cannon barrels.

In the 1800s, chemists searched for a clean-burning, smokeless explosive.

Christian Friedrich Schonbein was a German chemist born near Baden-Baden, a German town noted for its warm springs. He taught chemistry at Epsom, England. Like Baden-Baden, the town had springs with a mineral dissolved in it. Epsom salt from the spring was supposed to be good for a person's health. He investigated a compound of three oxygen atoms formed by an electric spark and named the compound ozone. Later, he moved to Basel, Switzerland, to teach at the university. Basel became a center of the Swiss chemical and drug manufacturing industries.

In 1846, Christian Schonbein experimented with nitric and sulfuric acids.

He was working at home in the kitchen. His wife had forbidden chemical experiments in the kitchen, but she was away and he planned to finish before her return. Christian Schonbein spilled some of the acid mixture. After he cleaned up the mess, he realized he had used his wife's apron. He quickly washed it out and hung it over the hot stove to dry.

Suddenly, the apron vanished in a flash of light. So complete was its destruction that not even smoke curled up from where the apron had been.

Schonbein could hardly overlook an exploding apron. He had accidentally made nitrocellulose, a combination of a nitrogen compound with cellulose. During the 1840s, organic chemists used cellulose as a raw material to make synthetic products. It was an organic compound from plants. Cellulose is found in the walls of plant cells. It bonds with other chemicals to give the cells their strong walls. Trees would sag under their own weight without the stiffening of the cell walls. Wood is a good source of cellulose. The best source is cotton. It is practically pure cellulose.

Nitrocellulose had been discovered earlier. By washing out the acid, Schonbein had improved its explosive properties. Schonbein named his discovery guncotton to call attention to its special properties. It was made from the cellulose in cotton, and he believed it could replace gunpowder. He showed the explosive to

Christian Friedrich Schonbein

people in several countries. He pointed out that it was three times more powerful than gunpowder, yet released practically no smoke. Here, he claimed, was the long-awaited smokeless gunpowder.

Countries rushed ahead with its manufacture. Soon they learned that guncotton was much too willing to explode. Chemists could carefully make a small amount in the laboratory. Factories could not safely produce it in quantity. When made properly, guncotton needed a spark or heat to set it off. Should the acid not be completely washed out, then it could explode without warning.

Businessmen decided that it was too unpredictable and refused to invest in the manufacture of guncotton. Later, chemists learned how to make the explosive more stable. By then, other explosives had been invented.

The year after guncotton came on the scene, an Italian inventor developed another explosive. Ascanio Sobrero added glycerin to a mixture of nitric acid and sulfuric acid. Glycerin is a thick, sweet-tasting organic compound. The mixture produced nitroglycerin. It, too, was a colorless, oily liquid. He heated it in a test tube and was nearly killed by the explosion.

When he set off nitroglycerin, it instantly produced about 12,000 times its own volume of gas at a temperature of 5000°C (9000°F). Four hot gases — carbon dioxide, water vapor, nitrogen gas, and oxygen gas — expanded outward with astonishing speed. Compared to black powder and guncotton, nitroglycerin was a high explosive. The gases expanded at a far faster rate.

The explosive power of nitroglycerin frightened Ascanio Sobrero. He only revealed his discovery to a small group of his chemist friends. He urged them to not make the explosive or try to sell it. For about ten years, he managed to keep the explosive secret.

Explosive merchants learned of Sobrero's discovery. In the 1850s, they tried to figure out a safe way to transport, store, and use it. Not only was nitroglycerin more explosive than guncotton, but it was a liquid rather than a solid. Jarring it could set it off as could heat, flame, or a static electric spark. If stored improperly, it could become unstable. The heat of a person's hand would be enough to cause

it to explode. For ten more years explosive merchants avoided nitroglycerin.

In the 1860s, two people dared to use nitroglycerin. They were the Swedish father and son team of Immanuel and Alfred Nobel. The Nobels sold nitroglycerin as blasting oil. Immanuel, the father, was the businessman and Alfred, the son, was the chemist. They sold it for use in mining and construction work. People used it for quarrying rock, blasting tunnels, digging canals, and making roadways.

Because of the transportation danger, they built manufacturing plants near where the construction would be done. Alfred would travel with the explosive and show how it could be used. One of these trips took him to the United States. The American president, Abraham Lincoln, had announced one of the greatest construction projects ever envisioned. He proposed to connect California to the East Coast with a

railroad. Building such a railroad would require removing rock and blasting tunnels through the Rocky Mountains. Nitroglycerin would replace the sweat of hours of manual labor with a single blast.

As the use of nitroglycerin increased, Alfred Nobel built in Sweden a modern factory where the dangerous chemical could be safely manufactured. He used the best available information and designed a factory that he believed to be safe. However, in 1864 his nitroglycerin factory exploded and killed five people, including his youngest brother Emil.

Alfred stopped further production. He built a floating laboratory on a barge in the middle of a lake. Should it explode, only he would suffer. He searched for a way to make nitroglycerin easier to transport and use. He became convinced the explosive would be safer as a solid. But what would absorb the thick liquid? He searched for the right medium.

Sticks of dynamite banded together increased nitroglycerin's explosive power.

Alfred Nobel found the answer in diatoms, tiny skeletons of sea life. Rather than having cell walls of cellulose, their cell walls were made of sand-like material, silica. Diatomaceous earth soaked up

nitroglycerin. Then he molded the moist paste into sticks. Alfred Nobel invented the name "dynamite" for his safer explosive. The word dynamite comes from a Greek word meaning "abundant power." It is the same word used to describe Christians in Luke 24:49.

Sticks of dynamite had few of the undesirable properties of liquid nitroglycerin. They could be carried safely, stored, transported, and used. The sticks could be banded together for greater power or broken in half for a smaller explosion. Miners and tunnel builders learned how to place charges to get the exact effect they wanted. Dynamite, like nitroglycerin, was smokeless.

Dynamite sticks normally would not even detonate unless used with a blasting cap. Alfred Nobel also invented the blasting cap. This device provided a dependable way to detonate nitroglycerin and other high explosives. Construction companies ordered dynamite. They safely blasted out foundations for buildings and bridges and carved out railroad beds and highways.

Alfred Nobel's skill as an inventor and businessman made him a fortune. He became a multi-millionaire.

In 1888, he had an upsetting experience. A newspaper publisher thought he had died and printed his death notice. The obituary described him as a merchant of death. It emphasized the sales of his explosive to the military where it was being used for bombs and other weapons.

Alfred Nobel did not want to be remembered in the way the newspaper had pictured him. He decided to prepare a will that would emphasize efforts to make the world a better place. He set aside money that would provide "prizes to those who, during the preceding year, shall have conferred the greatest benefit on mankind." He offered Nobel Prizes for physics, chemistry, medicine, literature, and peace. Later, the Nobel Committee added a prize for economics.

Nobel insisted that the prizes be international in scope. He wrote, "It is my express wish that in awarding the prizes no consideration whatever shall be given to the nationality of the candidates, but that the most worthy shall receive the prize."

Alfred Nobel died a year after making out his will. The first Nobel Prizes were awarded near the beginning of the century in 1901. The first winner of the chemistry prize was Jacobus H. van't Hoff. He was a chemist from the Netherlands who worked out the three-dimensional shapes of molecules.

At the end of the century in 1999, the Nobel Prize in chemistry was awarded to Professor Ahmed H. Zewail of the California Institute of Technology in Pasadena, California. He developed a way to use incredibly short flashes of light from laser beams to study chemical reactions in stop action.

Today, the Nobel Prizes are more famous than Alfred Nobel or his explosive made from nitroglycerin.

Nitroglycerin also has a medical use. Some people have a condition in which the blood vessels near the human heart thicken and harden. Blood cannot flow freely. Heart muscles do not receive enough oxygen. The muscles signal their distress to the brain. The victim experiences agonizing chest pains. Nitroglycerin tablets bring relief by relaxing the walls of the arteries. They open, and blood flows more freely. Once the heart muscles receive oxygen, this relieves the pain.

Nitrogen compounds are also used in fertilizers. When soils are worn out,

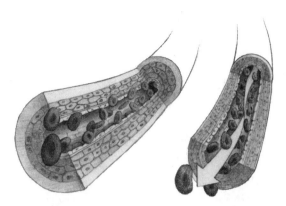

Nitroglycerin relaxes the walls of arteries helping blood to flow more freely.

fertilizers add essential elements to the soil. Plants grow healthier and produce better crops.

Some elements are more important than others. The four most abundant elements in living things are carbon, hydrogen, oxygen, and nitrogen. Where do plants get their essential elements? They take carbon from the carbon dioxide in the air. Hydrogen comes from water. Oxygen is readily available, either from water, carbon dioxide, or the air.

Nitrogen, however, is a problem. Nitrogen is the single most difficult element to replace in the soil. Yet, nitrogen itself is plentiful. The earth's atmosphere contains a vast storehouse of nitrogen. An abundant supply of compounds of that element would seem assured. That is not the case. Nitrogen gas from the atmosphere is practically inert. It seldom forms compounds. Plants cannot take it in directly from the air. Instead, they must extract it from the soil. Some soils lack enough nitrogen. Even rich topsoil can become exhausted after growing the same crops year after year.

One way to replace nitrogen-poor soil is to alternate crops. Corn and beans can remove nitrogen from the soil. Legumes such as peas, peanuts, alfalfa, or clover replace it. Legumes have nitrogen-fixing bacteria clustered in nodules about their roots. The bacteria capture nitrogen and combine it with other elements. They form nitrogen compounds that plants use as food.

Another way to replace nitrogen in poor soil is to use fertilizers. By the start of the 1900s, thedemand for nitrogen-based fertilizers outstripped the available supply. Most fertilizers came from naturally rich deposits. Countries guarded these natural fertilizer deposits as carefully as gold mines or oil fields. Bolivia and Chile fought a war over natural deposits of potassium nitrate in South America.

Chemists found that they could make nitrogen fertilizers from ammonia. Ammonia was a simple molecule of one nitrogen atom and three hydrogen atoms, NH_3. Such a simple compound should be easy to make — merely combine nitrogen from the air with hydrogen from water. Chemists looked for years for an easy way to make ammonia. No ordinary chemical reaction forced nitrogen and hydrogen together.

Success came to Fritz Haber, a German chemist, around 1911. He knew that he'd need a lot of energy to force nitrogen to share electrons with hydrogen. He carried the reaction out at a high temperature, 600°C (about 1100°F). To force the atoms closer together, he used an incredibly high pressure, 700 times normal atmospheric pressure. The reaction took place at a very slow rate.

He found that finely divided iron particles speeded the reaction.

The Haber process gives ammonia. Millions of tons of ammonia go into fertilizers each year. Plants absorb fertilizers and are harvested for food. Your body probably contains several million nitrogen atoms that began in the food chain through the Haber process. Fritz Haber won the Nobel Prize in chemistry in 1918.

REACTION

1. **Nitrogen compounds made powerful explosives.**

2. **Alfred Nobel made dynamite, a safer, solid form of nitroglycerine.**

3. **Nobel began the Nobel prizes to recognize achievements in science. There is a peace prize, also.**

1. The essential element in explosives is _____.

A-B 2. The powder in the expression "keep your powder dry" was (A. diatomaceous earth; B. gunpowder).

T F 3. The rapid expansion of hot gases causes the destruction of an explosion.

T F 4. Gunpowder is smokeless.

5. Nitrocellulose is a combination of a _____ compound with cellulose.

A-D 6. Cellulose gives plant cells their (A. ability to do photosynthesis; B. color; C. daily supply of water; D. strong cell walls).

A-D 7. The one that is practically pure cellulose is (A. cotton; B. diamond; C. silicon dioxide; D. protein).

A-B 8. Guncotton would be described as being (A. a safe and effective explosive; B. unpredictable and capable of exploding without warning).

A-B 9. Ascanio Sobrero's reaction to nitroglycerin was to (A. announce its discovery at a chemical congress; B. keep it secret).

T F 10. The Nobels sold nitroglycerin as blasting oil.

A-D 11. Abraham Lincoln's great construction project was to connect California to the East Coast with (A. an interstate highway; B. a pony express route; C. a railroad; D. a telegraph line).

T F 12. Alfred Nobel's nitroglycerin factory in Sweden proved to be completely safe.

A-D 13. Diatoms have cell walls of (A. cellulose; B. dynamite; C. nitroglycerin; D. silica).

A-D 14. Blasting caps are used (A. for safe detonation of explosives; B. for small explosions; C. to contain an explosion; D. to control the direction of an explosion).

T F 15. The upsetting event that Alfred Nobel experienced was reading his own death notice in the newspaper.

T F 16. Nobel prizes can only be awarded to the citizens of Sweden.

T F 17. Nitrogen compounds are used in fertilizers.

Silicon and Its Compounds

Silicon is the second most abundant element in the earth's crust, behind oxygen. The name silicon is from *silex*, a Latin word meaning "flint." Flint is a rock made of silicon and oxygen. Silicon's chemical symbol is Si.

Silicon is below carbon in the periodic table and has properties similar to those of carbon. Silicon in the form of a crystal has its atoms arranged in the same pyramid-like structure as carbon atoms in diamond. Silicon is not as hard as diamond. Silicon atoms are larger than carbon atoms and do not pack together as tightly.

A combination of silicon and carbon does produce an exceedingly hard material. Silicon carbide, SiC, is a synthetic compound first made

A C T I O N

1. Quartz withstood rapid changes in temperatures.

2. Colored glass was easier to make than perfectly clear glass.

3. Temperature changes severely affected motor oils.

4. Silicon is neither a good conductor of electricity nor a good insulator of electricity.

Can You Predict the Reactions?

during trials to produce synthetic diamond. The American chemist Edward Goodrich Acheson worked at Thomas A. Edison's laboratories. When Acheson heated carbon with clay, the result was a substance almost as hard as diamond. Tests showed that it had the structure of diamond, but with half of the carbon atoms replaced by silicon.

Acheson's silicon carbide crystal did not have the beauty of diamond. However, it was a useful product for grinding. Mineralogists use it today to smooth precious stones and gems. They place the stones in a container with water and silicon carbide. Several weeks of tumbling gives the stones a smooth surface.

Silicon makes up more than one-fourth of the earth's crust by weight. The crust is the top part of the earth, the part scientists know best. Oxygen and silicon together make up three-fourths of the earth's rocky surface.

Silica is the simplest compound of silicon and oxygen. Silica is silicon dioxide, SiO_2. The silicon and oxygen atoms lock together in pyramid-like arrangement. Chemists find it everywhere in the earth's crust. Quartz is the most abundant silica mineral and the purest. Grains of white sand are mostly small crystals of pure quartz. White sand also forms from gypsum and broken seashells.

Chemists melt quartz and shape it into test tubes, beakers, and other laboratory utensils. Quartz can withstand rapid changes in temperature. When heated, quartz expands much less than glass. For the same temperature rise, the expansion of quartz is only 1/18th that of glass. Glass contracts unevenly when exposed to sudden temperature changes. The strain causes the glass to shatter. Quartz is more resistant to temperature extremes.

You can heat quartz red hot and plunge it into cold water without damage to it. Chemists use quartz for beakers and test tubes that must undergo severe temperature changes.

Astronomical telescopes use mirrors to reflect light to a focus. The mirrors are usually made of glass coated with aluminum. As astronomers made reflecting telescopes larger and larger, a serious problem arose. Heat causes glass to expand, and cold causes it to contract. A thick slab of glass such as a telescope mirror expanded unevenly. Even slight changes in temperature set up internal strains. The glass warped, giving poor images in the telescope.

A telescope mirror of quartz is much more stable than one of glass. It does not warp, so it gives a higher quality

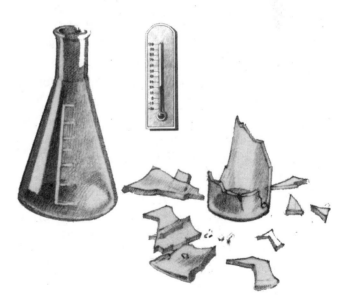

Quartz vs. Glass

image. The only drawback is the cost. The effort to melt quartz and form it into shape is costly. Scientists use it only for instruments where they cannot control the temperature.

Quartz has an unusual electrical property. When a crystal of quartz is squeezed, such as in the jaws of pliers, it will generate a small spark. Releasing the pressure causes another small electric charge.

The electric effect goes the other way, too. Sending a small electric current through a quartz crystal makes it expand and contract. Each crystal has a natural rate of vibration. By cutting crystals to the proper size, scientists can tune them to vibrate at a set frequency. The rate is very precise and predictable. Watches, radios, and televisions all have quartz crystals as internal clocks to keep them running on time.

Glass, like quartz, contains silicon. Chemists make ordinary window glass by melting sand with limestone and soda ash. For many centuries, glassmakers struggled to form perfectly clear glass. Instead, impurities colored the glass. Glassmakers chose to hide their imperfections by intentionally coloring their glass. They did this by mixing in metal oxides such as cobalt or lead. Glass that has been colored in this way is known as stained glass.

Today visitors marvel at the beauty of stained glass windows in old churches. A few hundred years ago, people would have been amazed at large sheets of perfectly clear glass. Clear picture windows would have been a wonder to them.

Glass has no definite freezing or melting point. Unlike quartz with its definite crystalline form, glass has no fixed internal structure. As glass is heated, it becomes soft like butter. When it

Stained glass

cools again, it at first acts as a very slow-moving liquid. Finally, it changes into a solid.

Glass is an example of a silicate, a compound of silicon, oxygen, and a metal. Silicon and oxygen form the basic structure of a silicate. A silicate also contains a metallic element such as alminum, iron, manganese, or sodium. Most construction materials, such as glass, ceramic, brick, concrete, and building stones are silicates. The range of silicate properties is vast. Soft talcum powder is made from talc, a silicate. Beautiful and hard emerald is a silicate.

Many precious gems such as emerald, amethyst, agate, jasper, and opal also contain silica, silicon dioxide. Opal is the most valuable silicate gem. It is translucent and has an iridescent star-like luster.

A gem must be hard to withstand wear, polish to a high gloss to look attractive, and show a pleasing color.

Most gems appear even more attractive when properly displayed. Grinding, polishing, and putting the gem in a setting adds to its value. A gem's value is a combination of cost, beauty, and rarity.

In some cases, the history of a stone adds to its value. One of the best-known gems is the Star of India sapphire. Sapphire is an aluminum oxide. It was found in Ceylon (now Sri Lanka) and purchased by J.P. Morgan. It is now in the American Museum of Natural History in New York City.

Another well-known gem is the Hope Diamond. It was found in India and purchased in 1668 by Louis XIV as one of the crown jewels of France. The original stone was 112 carats. A carat is a measure of weight. It takes 142 carats to weigh an ounce. It was cut into a heart shape in 1673 that reduced it to 67 carats. It disappeared in 1792 following the confusion of the French Revolution. In 1830, London banker Thomas Hope purchased a 45.5 carat diamond that many believe was cut

The Hope Diamond

from the original diamond. Today, the Hope Diamond is on display in the Smithsonian Institution, Washington, D.C. The final Hope Diamond is less than one-half the size of the original stone.

The value of a gem can change dramatically. Amethyst, for instance, is a form of quartz with manganese as an impurity. It has a purple or violet color. At one time in Europe, people highly prized amethyst as a gemstone. When Europeans learned of large deposits of amethyst in Brazil in South America, the price plunged. Today, people class the pretty gem as semiprecious.

Most gems are impure. Sometimes the impurities give the gem its unique properties. For instance, cat's eye is a quartz-based gem that contains fibers of asbestos. Asbestos is a mineral that has fibers that can be woven like cloth. At one time, asbestos was used as a fire resistant material, but its use has been limited because of health concerns. Cat's eye displays a band of reflected light that shifts position as you view it from different angles.

The Star of India

Chemists have learned how to make synthetic silicate gems. A synthetic gem is one that has the same properties as one found in nature. A synthetic gem is not a fake gem. The difference is that fake gems are made of some cheap material such as glass that has been cut to look like a gem. Usually, the synthetic gem is more regular and does not have the imperfections of the natural variety.

The first synthetic gem was a ruby. In the early 1800s, chemists mixed a powder of chromium oxide and aluminum oxide. Oxygen gas carried the powder and was burned with hydrogen. The reaction took place inside a hot furnace. A pear-shaped ruby formed at the end of the gas nozzle. A ruby cut from the droplet was as brilliant as the natural variety.

One characteristic of a gem is hardness. Rubies are hard and have low friction. They became widely used in mechanical watches as bearings for the moving parts. In the 1960s, ruby rods were the heart of visible light lasers.

Silicone is a silicon material made in the laboratory. Silicones are the silicon equivalents to hydrocarbons. Rather than a backbone of carbon atoms, silicones have a backbone of silicon atoms alternating with oxygen atoms. Silicones can be oily liquids, heavy lubri-

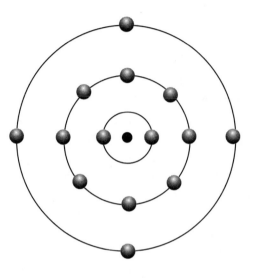

Electronic configuration of silicon atom

cants, or rubber-like putty. They have many uses. Regular hydrocarbon motor oils are thick like molasses on cold mornings. They become thin when the engine runs at high speed and warms up. Aircraft engines can become even hotter, causing the hydrocarbon chains to break apart. The damaged oil no longer protects engines from friction. In the 1940s, chemists learned that silicones can replace lubricating oil in aircraft engines. Unlike regular oils, heat and cold hardly affect silicone oils. Silicone oils lubricate regardless of the temperature.

Silicone rubber also can withstand harsh conditions. Hoses and tubes of silicone rubber stay flexible even in freezing temperatures. Many of the

Silicone rubber gives hoses and tubing their flexibilty.

From solar panels
to transistor radios,
silicone has many uses.

hoses and tubes of aircraft and flight suits for pilots are of silicone rubber.

Despite its many important uses, most people know silicone best as an amusing toy, Silly-Putty. This is the brand name of a compound made of long chains that contain silicon. You can roll it into sheets, stretch it into strips, or draw it into taffy-like threads. You must do it slowly. If you strike it sharply with a hammer, it will shatter. If you pull it briskly, it snaps. If rolled into a ball and thrown against a hard wall it bounces back like a rubber ball.

What explains these contradictory properties? Long chains of molecules make silicones. These long molecules twist and intertwine with one another. Given time, the chains sort themselves out. If snapped quickly, the chains resist the action. They break.

Like carbon, silicon has many compounds. Silicon compounds differ widely from one another. Some are hard like quartz and flint. Others are soft like asbestos and talc. People have used these compounds in daily life for centuries. Pure silicon, however, had few applications until the 1950s. Pure silicon never occurs naturally in the free state.

Instead, chemists find it combined with some other element, usually oxygen. A chemist can remove the oxygen to give a crystal of silicon.

Most non-metals are electric insulators. They are poor conductors of electricity. Metals are electric conductors. They provide a ready path for an electric current. Silicon, however, doesn't conduct very well, but it doesn't insulate against electric flow either. Silicon and germanium (below it in the periodic table) are semiconductors.

Chemists learned to make silicon crystals with carefully controlled impurities. The impurities caused dramatic changes in silicon's electric properties. Until the 1950s, most radios and other electric devices depended upon vacuum tubes to regulate and amplify electric currents. In 1948, William Shockley, an American physicist, made silicon crystals with impurities of arsenic and gallium.

Silicon is used in
computer chip technology.

the central processing unit, the CPU. Many home computers have CPUs of more than a million silicon devices. They are on a chip as small as a postage stamp.

It is interesting that the primary element in the human brain is carbon, while the primary element in a computer is silicon. Both are members of the same chemical family and have similar properties.

Modern home computers have more than a million silicon devices.

His silicon semiconductors amplified radio waves far better than vacuum tubes.

Silicon's replacement of vacuum tubes to amplify electric current opened a vast number of uses for the element. Silicon goes into solar cells, transistors for radios, and silicon chips for computers. Silicon has given its name to Silicon Valley, an area in California noted for its many computer firms.

At first, electric devices had individual components made of silicon chips. Later, chip manufacturers learned to put hundreds of diodes, transistors, and computer processing units on a single chip. The individual components are microscopic in size. An integrated circuit in a simple calculator may contain as many as 50,000 parts. These fit on a small silicon chip less than a millimeter square. The main brain of a computer is

REACTION

1. **Chemists use quartz for laboratory beakers and test tubes.**

2. **Stained glass hid the imperfections while clear glass contained no impurities.**

3. **Silicone oils remained unchanged despite vast temperature changes.**

4. **Semiconductor silicon chips replaced vacuum tubes to make miniature electronic equipment.**

A-B 1. Silicon is the (A. most abundant; B. second most abundant) element in the earth's crust.

A-D 2. Silicon carbide was discovered while trying to make synthetic (A. diamond; B. glass; C. rubies; D. Silly-Putty).

A-B 3. The one that can resist sudden changes in temperature is (A. glass; B. quartz).

T F 4. Electricity passing through a quartz crystal causes it to expand and contract.

A-D 5. Stained glass was colored (A. because church officials did not want people to look outside during church services; B. to hide the fact that glass makers could not make clear glass; C. to prevent it from melting; D. because people did not like clear glass).

A-D 6. A gem's value is due to its (A. beauty; B. cost; C. rarity; D. all of the above).

A-D 7. The Star of India is (A. a diamond; B. a sapphire; C. a synthetic ruby; D. an opal).

T F 8. The Hope Diamond was cut and recut until it was less than half the size of the original stone.

T F 9. A synthetic gem is a fake gem.

A-B 10. The one better able to lubricate across extreme temperatures is (A. hydrocarbon motor oil; B. silicone oil).

T F 11. Silly-putty is made of long chain-like molecules that contain silicon.

A-D 12. Silicon is an electric (A. conductor; B. insulator; C. semiconductor; D. none of the above).

A-B 13. The element found in computer chips is (A. carbon; B. silicon).

Modern Metals

Aluminum is a modern metal. It did not come into use until the middle of the 1800s. Before then, the chief metals were those that had been known since ancient times: gold, silver, copper, iron, tin, lead, and mercury. Others metals such as zinc were used for making alloys. Platinum, discovered in the 1500s, found some use as a coinage metal. However, people continued to use the seven ancient metals until the discovery of aluminum. Today, aluminum is the second-most widely used metal after iron.

Aluminum is the most abundant metallic element in the earth's crust. Only oxygen and silicon are more abundant and they are nonmetals. Clay contains aluminum as does bauxite, its main ore. About eight percent of the earth's crust by weight is aluminum. Bauxite is even richer in aluminum. The best grade of bauxite is about 35 percent alu-

ACTION

1. **Although common, aluminum was difficult to separate from bauxite ore.**

2. **Photographic film left in a desk became fogged as if exposed to light.**

3. **Pitchblende was radioactive even after the uranium was removed.**

Can You Predict the Reactions?

Hans Christian Øersted

minum by weight. Despite being so common, separating aluminum from clay or bauxite is not easy.

In the early 1800s, Danish chemist Hans Christian Øersted became the first to produce aluminum. Chemists refined most metals by heating with carbon. Iron was separated from its ore in that way. Humphry Davy used electricity to refine metals such as sodium. Aluminum holds very firmly to oxygen. Neither heating with carbon nor electricity would pry aluminum atoms away from oxygen.

Hans Christian Øersted began with clay, which contained aluminum. He mixed clay with charcoal, heated the mixture white hot, and steamed it with chlorine gas. Then he added potassium and mercury and heated it again. He got a very poor grade of aluminum. Øersted could tell enough about the element to see that it was a metal and had a luster similar to that of tin.

Aluminum remained a laboratory curiosity with no commercial value. In 1855, a French chemist freed marble-sized pellets of aluminum. The process was expensive. Aluminum cost more than silver. France's Emperor Napoleon III ordered a table set of the expensive metal. At a banquet his honored guests ate with aluminum spoons and forks. Less important officials had to make do with gold and silver cutlery.

In America, people collected money to build a monument to George Washington. They ordered a solid aluminum cap for the tall stone monument. It weighed six pounds. Construction was delayed because of lack of funds and the Civil War. The Monument Committee put the aluminum pyramid on display. Visitors jumped over it. Later, they could claim to have jumped over the top of the Washington Monument. Construction resumed in 1878. Six years later the Washington Monument was topped out with its expensive aluminum cap.

A chemistry student at Oberlin College in Ohio read news reports about the aluminum top to the Washington Monument. His college instructor

The Washington Monument

reviewed the information known about the metal and made a prediction. The professor said, "The chemist who finds a cheap way to refine aluminum will become world famous and wealthy."

Charles Martin Hall decided to try it. He built a laboratory in his woodshed. He began by repeating the work of others, especially those experiments that sent electricity through aluminum ore. For electricity to free aluminum, the ore needed to be molten. That took a high temperature. In one experiment, he heated crystals of cryolite until they melted. Cryolite was a compound of fluorine, sodium, and aluminum. Cryolite melted at a far lower temperature than aluminum ore. Best of all, aluminum ore dissolved in the molten cryolite.

Charles Hall passed an electric current through the molten mixture. Pure aluminum collected at one of the electrical terminals. He rushed to his professor with the first few samples of the metal. He quickly made plans to patent the process. He knew that aluminum had many desirable features. It weighed about 2.7 times an equal volume of water. It was strong, did not corrode or rust, and could be combined with other metals to make lightweight but strong building material.

In France, another young chemist, Paul Héroult, developed essentially the same process. Paul had been a few months earlier in his discovery, but had not realized its importance and did not patent his process as quickly. Although Hall had claims to the American patent, Héroult had the European rights to aluminum.

It looked like the story of aluminum would bog down into a long and costly court battle. Instead, Charles Martin Hall and Paul Héroult became friends. They decided to pool their knowledge and improve the process. They made aluminum so cheaply that it began to rival iron as a building material. Within two years of being placed on the top of the Washington Monument, the value of the aluminum in the cap had decreased to 1/1000th of its original price.

Charles Martin Hall never forgot the Ohio school that set him on the road to discovery. He set aside five million dollars for Oberlin College. He and Paul Héroult were born in the same year, 1863, and died the same year, 1914.

Their process was a commercial success. It is still used today to refine aluminum from bauxite. Aluminum is cheap enough to use for everyday purposes. Pots and pans are made of it. Homes have siding of aluminum. Drinks come in aluminum cans. Aluminum foil wraps food in place of tin.

Like most metals, aluminum is malleable. It can be rolled into thin sheets. A sheet of aluminum foil is about 1/100th of an inch thick. At one time, tin foil was used to wrap foods, especially chocolates. Today, aluminum foil has replaced tin for this purpose.

Aluminum foil is used for countless applications. During the early days of space exploration, the United States launched several large balloons into orbit. They were made of plastic coated with aluminum. Rocket scientists folded the balloons down to fit in containers only 40 inches in diameter. Once in orbit around the earth, a small amount of gas inflated them to 135 feet in diameter. Radio engineers used the satellites to bounce radio waves back to earth. They were called echo satellites.

Aluminum-coated, fire-resistant suits protect fire fighters from extreme temperature.

Aluminum is a good conductor of electricity. Only gold, silver, and copper are better conductors. To conduct the same amount of electricity as copper wires, aluminum wires must be made thicker. Even with the greater size, they are lighter than copper and do not cost as much. High-voltage cross-country electric lines are made of aluminum.

One interesting use of aluminum is as emergency shelters for fighters of forest fires. Should the wind change direction, firefighters can be caught in a fast-moving firestorm. These deadly blazes pass through an area in just minutes. During that short time, the temperature rises to several hundred degrees. Firefighters carry a packet with a folded blanket inside. The blanket is made of several layers of aluminum and fireproof fabric. If trapped by a blaze, they seek shelter under the tent-like blanket. Because aluminum reflects heat, the temperature inside the shelter stays cool enough for the firefighter to survive.

Freeing aluminum from oxygen requires a lot of energy. The opposite reaction — allowing aluminum to combine with oxygen — releases great quantities of heat. A combination of powdered aluminum and iron oxide is known as thermite. The iron oxide contains oxygen, which will react with aluminum. When thermite is ignited, a spectacular reaction results. Thermite gets very hot indeed. The temperature of a thermite reaction is about 2,400°C (4,400°F).

The thermite reaction is hot enough to melt iron. The reaction is used for spot welding of heavy equipment at remote construction sites. It is also used to weld together sections of railroad tracks. A container of thermite is placed over the seam between the two sections of track and ignited. The iron melts, fills the seam, and when it cools the sections are welded together. The thermite reaction is vigorous enough to burn underwater. Divers can weld broken ship propellers underwater.

Uranium is another of the modern metals. Most periodic tables of the elements show two rows along the bottom of the chart. Chemists call these series of elements rare earth elements. Despite the names, the rare earth elements are metals. They often occur in the same ore. Chemists find it difficult to separate one from another.

In the late 1700s, German chemist Martin Klaproth tested a dark, heavy mineral called pitchblende. He treated the mineral with a strong acid. From it, he extracted a yellow powder. He concluded that it was a metal combined with oxygen. Martin Klaproth never did extract the metal. Klaproth could find no particular use for the powder. He feared his discovery would sink from the public eye. He searched for some way to give his new metal publicity.

A few years earlier, William Herschel had discovered a new planet, the first one found in modern times. The new planet orbited beyond Saturn, so astronomers named it Uranus after the father of Saturn. Martin Klaproth decided to name his metal after the planet. He called it uranium. Despite Martin Klaproth's best efforts, uranium faded into obscurity.

This changed in 1896. Invisible and very penetrating x-rays had been discovered in that year. They were produced when high-speed electrons struck a metal target. Henri Becquerel, a French physicist, wondered if fluorescent crystals could produce x-rays if exposed to sunlight. He took photographic film and wrapped it in heavy, dark paper so light wouldn't expose the

Henri Becquerel

film. Then he put a fluorescent crystal on the wrapped film and set it in the sunlight.

Suppose the crystals gave off x-rays. They would go through the paper and fog the film. Cloudy weather cut the experiment short. Becquerel set aside the film without developing it. The clouds stayed around for several days, so Becquerel decided to develop the film anyway. Sunlight had struck the crystal for only a few minutes. He expected the film to be clear.

He held up the film, amazed. It had darkened as if exposed to light. What could have caused it? Had something in his desk exposed the film? He wrapped another sheet of film and put it in his desk. After a time it fogged, too. Becquerel had many rocks and minerals in his desk. One by one he eliminated them. The source of the fogging rays came from pitchblende, the uranium ore.

Becquerel announced his incredible finding. He said, "Uranium emits invisible rays as powerful as x-rays."

At an unpredictable moment, a uranium atom broke apart. It shot out high-speed electrons, alpha particles, and gamma rays. Gamma rays have more energy than x-rays. They exposed photographic film tightly wrapped in paper as easily as if the film were exposed to sunlight.

Could other radioactive elements exist? Two of Becquerel's friends, Pierre Curie and his wife Marie, decided to answer the question. They removed all the uranium from the ore. Oddly enough, pitchblende seemed to be more radioactive with the metal removed. Chemists had carefully separated the elements in pitchblende. None of them were radioactive.

What could explain the Curies' discovery? They decided pitchblende contained an element in such small amounts it had escaped detection. Yet, the small amount of material had to be intensely radioactive, even more so than uranium.

In 1898, the Curies separated a second radioactive metal from pitchblende. They called it polonium. Marie named it after her home country of Poland. The symbol is Po.

Polonium and uranium together did not completely explain the radioactivity of pitchblende. Still another radioactive element had to be present. The Curies gave the mystery element the name radium. They set out to isolate a sample of it from pitchblende. Marie arranged for eight tons of the ore to be delivered to their workshop. They spent four years separating the radium. Their hard work yielded 1/10 of a gram of radium, a speck about the size of a pinhead.

Radium was so radioactive it glowed in the dark. It was 100 million times more radioactive than an equal amount of pure uranium. In 1903, Pierre and Marie Curie received the Nobel Prize in physics. They shared it with Henri Becquerel. Later, Marie Curie received a second Nobel Prize in 1911 in chemistry.

Uranium has an atomic number of 92. It is the last of the naturally occurring elements. Elements beyond uranium, those with atomic numbers greater than 92, do exist. Nuclear scientists make them by bombarding uranium with neutrons and other atomic particles. Uranium atoms capture the neutrons, undergo a nuclear change, and become atoms of the heavier elements. All elements beyond uranium are radioactive. An atom of any of these elements will sooner or later undergo radioactive decay.

The Curies discover radium.

Chemists gave the first element beyond uranium the name neptunium, Np. Neptune is the planet next after Uranus and neptunium is the element after uranium. The next element is plutonium, named after the planet Pluto. Nuclear reactors produce plutonium. It is used to power heart pacemakers, a device that causes the heart to beat with a regular rhythm.

You probably have another radioactive element in your home. The next element after plutonium is americium, named after America. Americium is an essential part of smoke detectors. When smoke particles are in the air, fewer radioactive rays from americium reach the detector. An electric circuit senses a change in the number of

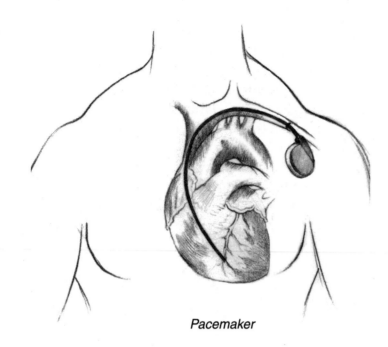

Pacemaker

rays reaching the detector and sets off the smoke alarm.

Other elements beyond uranium were named after states and cities. Californium is named after the state of California. And berkelium is named after the city of Berkeley, California. The ending ium shows that the elements are metals. Some new elements are named after people. Element #101, mendelevium is named after Dmitri Mendeleev. Element #102 nobelium is named after Alfred Nobel. It has been proposed that element #109 meitnerium is named for Lise Meitner, a woman physicist who was primarily responsible for the discovery of nuclear fission.

New radioactive elements continued to be named after people and places up to element number 109. Elements beyond 109 have been detected but they have been given names and symbols that are based on their atomic number. Element number 110 is ununnilium. The word is a combination of un-un-nil-ium. The syllables mean one-one-zero with ium showing that it is a

metal. The symbol is Uun. The elements beyond 110 are the only ones with three letters as their symbols.

The last element synthesized before the start of the year 2000 was element number 118, named ununoctium. The syllables un-un-oct-ium mean one-one-eight with ium showing that it is a metal. Ununoctium was discovered in 1999 at the University of California at Berkeley. It has an atomic weight of 293, and the symbol is Uuo.

The ancient dream of changing one element into another is possible by exposing existing elements to radioactive particles. These discoveries of modern chemists are far more wonderful than merely changing lead into gold. These new metals can detect smoke and warn us of fires or power pacemakers to keep the human heart beating.

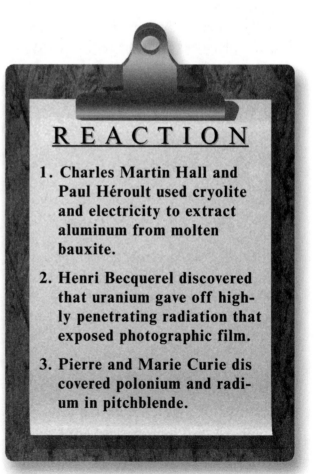

REACTION

1. **Charles Martin Hall and Paul Héroult used cryolite and electricity to extract aluminum from molten bauxite.**

2. **Henri Becquerel discovered that uranium gave off highly penetrating radiation that exposed photographic film.**

3. **Pierre and Marie Curie discovered polonium and radium in pitchblende.**

T F   1.   Aluminum is a rare element in the earth's crust.

T F   2.   Aluminum is the second most widely used metal after iron.

A-D   3.   France's Emperor Napoleon III had table sets made of (A. aluminum; B. copper; C. frozen nitrogen; D. uranium).

A-D   4.   The six-pound metallic top to the Washington Monument is made of (A. aluminum; B. gold; C. silver; D. uranium).

T F   5.   The commercial production of aluminum was delayed for several years because of a court battle between Paul Héroult and Charles Martin Hall.

A-D   6.   The foil used to wrap foods is made of (A. aluminum; B. steel; C. copper; D. zinc).

T F   7.   Aluminum is a better conductor of electricity than any other metal.

T F   8.   Aluminum reflects heat.

T F   9.   Thermite can burn under water.

A-B   10.   The one discovered first was the (A. planet Uranus; B. element uranium).

A-D   11.   Uranium ore is (A. galena; B. hematite; C. pitchblende; D. sulfur dioxide).

T F   12.   Polonium and radium are both radioactive.

T F   13.   Curie was refused a Nobel prize because she was a woman.

A-D   14.   The radioactive element used in smoke detectors is (A. americium; B. curium; C. radium; D. uranium).

T F   15.   Some elements beyond uranium were named after states and cities.

Chemistry in Today's World

This book has explored the key discoveries of chemistry. Who can resist making a list of the top ten chemists? A brief biography is given below of ten of the greatest chemists of all time. Others may decide in favor of one chemist over another for this list. However, there is agreement that these chemists are of the first rank. Their order is by their date of birth.

Robert Boyle (1627–1691) was the English chemist who saw the need for scientists to communicate their ideas quickly. He urged his fellow scientists to report their results so others might benefit from their discoveries. He helped start the Royal Society, a formal scientific body that met every week to exchange ideas.

Boyle proved that air is not a mysterious substance. Like solids and gases it follows natural laws. In his book *Touching the Spring of the Air,* he stated

ACTION

1. People working alone made chemical discoveries.

2. People working as teams made chemical discoveries.

3. People working in other fields made chemical discoveries.

   Can You Predict the Reactions?

that the volume of a gas varies inversely to the pressure.

He discovered the element phosphorus. It burst into flames when heated by friction. He used it to make the first match. His modern definition of an element put chemistry on a firm scientific footing. He defined an element as a substance that cannot be chemically separated into other elements and cannot be produced by combining two or more elements. His book *The Sceptical Chemist* marked the beginning of modern chemistry.

Robert Boyle was a humble Christian and a student of the Bible. He learned Hebrew and Greek to pursue his study of Scripture. He believed science offered another way to discover more about God and His creation. Robert Boyle said, "From a knowledge of His work, we shall know Him." When he died, his will set aside money for a yearly lecture defending Christianity against attacks by unbelievers.

Henry Cavendish (1731–1810) experimented with gases and was the first to measure their densities. In 1776 he discovered hydrogen when he released it by treating metals with hydrochloric acid. He is best known for his measurement of the tiny gravitational attraction between two bodies of ordinary size.

Cavendish was an eccentric person who ordered his servants to stay out of sight. Many of his papers did not become known until more than 50 years after his death. His work was useful even at that late date because it helped confirm discoveries that were just then being made.

Antoine Laurent Lavoisier (1743–1794) was a handsome and personally engaging French chemist. An interest in rocks and minerals led him into a study of chemistry and away from his father's profession as a lawyer. Lavoisier made measurement an essential part of chemistry. He borrowed a precision balance from the

French mint. Chemists believed prolonged boiling changed water into solid residue. Lavoisier boiled water in a closed container for more than a hundred days. Carefully weighing the container both before and after the experiment proved that the weight had not changed.

In another experiment, he burned a diamond in a closed container. Although the carbon in diamond changed into carbon dioxide by combining with the oxygen in the container, the total weight did not change. Lavoisier stated the law of conservation of matter: matter can neither be created nor destroyed during chemical change.

In one of his books, Lavoisier listed all of the known elements. He listed five substances that were not elements, including soda ash and potash. He believed they contained elements that chemists had not yet been able to separate from the compounds. Humphry Davy used this list in his search for elements.

Lavoisier invested money with his wife's father who ran a company that collected taxes for the government. In 1793 during the French Revolution, the fate of the country fell into the hands of the revolutionaries. Lavoisier was arrested as a tax collector. He was tried, convicted, and sentenced to death. He was executed by the guillotine on the same day as his trial.

John Dalton (1766–1844) was a Quaker. For most of his life, he earned a living as a teacher or tutor. John Dalton was color-blind and he made the first scientific study of the condition. He collected marsh gas (methane) and showed that it was made of carbon and hydrogen. Dalton's most important contribution to chemistry was his atomic theory. He proposed that all matter was made of individual particles that could not be divided by chemical reactions. Atoms of the same element were identical and had the same weight. Atoms of different elements were different in their properties, especially their weights.

John Dalton's atomic theory was not based upon idle speculation. Instead, he based it on experiments. He answered criticism of his theory so gently that he overcame all objections. The atomic theory was quickly accepted and became the single most important principle of chemistry.

Humphry Davy (1778–1829) moved chemistry into a modern era by introducing electricity as a means of refining new elements. He discovered potassium, sodium, barium, strontium, calcium, and magnesium. Davy's chemical career began early. While still a teenager, he was employed by

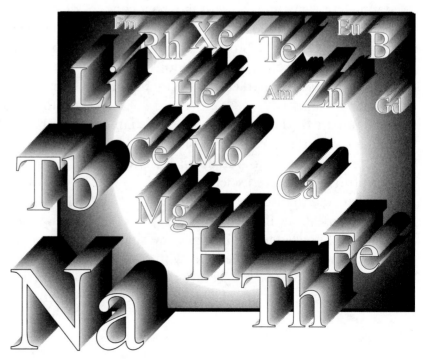

a clinic to test the medical uses of gases. He had the bad habit of sniffing and tasting chemicals. His life was probably shortened by his lack of caution. When asked his greatest discovery, he said, "Michael Faraday." It was a reference to his hiring the great chemist Michael Faraday as an assistant.

Jöns Jakob Berzelius (1779–1848) was a Swedish chemist. Although trained to be a physician, he became interested in the chemical composition of the drugs he prescribed. He analyzed 2,000 compounds from about 1807 to 1817. His work established the law of definite proportions: elements making a particular compound are always present in the same proportion. He prepared the first accurate table of atomic weights. The list helped Mendeleev reveal the periodic law.

Berzelius discovered three elements: cerium, selenium, and thorium. He freely gave advice to others. For more than 35 years, he published a yearly summary of advances in chemistry and suggested areas that needed further investigation. One of Berzelius' most useful suggestions was to represent the chemical elements by simply one and two letter abbreviations rather than drawings or other symbols.

Michael Faraday (1791–1867) began his career as a chemist in the employ of Humphry Davy. The only formal education he had received was at a church Sunday school. His belief in a Creator led him to search for unity in nature. Eventually, he showed how electricity, magnetism, and light were related.

Chemists had learned that electricity passing through a solution would free metals in the solution. Michael Faraday discovered laws that related the amount of metals to the amount of electricity. He also explained the operation of a battery. In chemistry, Faraday discovered the carbon compound benzene that later became important in the synthetic production of dyes and perfumes.

Despite his accomplishments, Faraday chose a simple life. He and his wife, Sarah, lived in an attic apartment above his laboratory. He never patented his inventions, but instead supported himself on the small

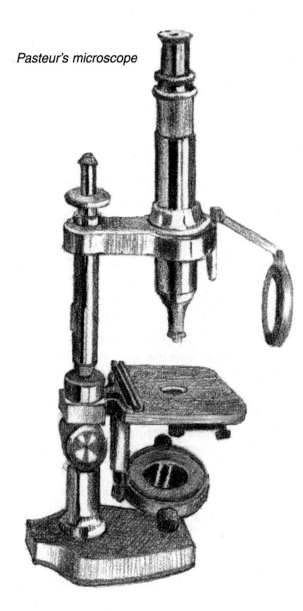

Pasteur's microscope

salary from the Royal Institution of Great Britain. During his early years, he had longed to learn more of science but was too poor to attend science lectures. In later life, he gave free talks at Christmas about science. He published one of the first science books written in a simple language that children could understand.

Michael Faraday believed that the Bible contained perfect truth. He said, "The Bible, and it alone, with nothing added to it or nothing taken from it by man, is the sole and sufficient guide for each individual, at all times and in all circumstances."

Louis Pasteur (1822–1895), a French chemist, is better known today for his medical researches. However, he began his career as a chemist. One of his first triumphs was to show that chemical molecules could exist as optical isomers. These molecules are mirror images of one another. Through a microscope, he saw that a mold consumed one type of food but ignored the other. His expertise with a microscope helped him solve the mystery of fermentation. Everyone believed fermentation was strictly a chemical process. However, he showed that small microorganisms produced fermentation.

Dmitri Ivanovich Mendeleev (1834–1907) discovered that properties of chemical elements repeat in a predictable way and summarized those properties in a periodic chart of the elements. His periodic chart of the elements is a powerful example of the order that is in nature, an order put there by the Creator. The periodic law is

Helium-filled balloons rise high into the atmosphere.

one of the most useful discoveries in chemistry. It helps make sense of the often confusing properties of the elements. Mendeleev also wrote a textbook, *The Principles of Chemistry,* for Russian students. It was translated into several other languages. Mendeleev lived in czarist Russia. He did not endear himself to the authorities because of his support of students. Element number 101, discovered in 1955 by American nuclear chemists, was named mendelevium in his honor.

William Ramsay (1852–1916) was a Christian who encouraged others to become followers of Jesus. He has the honor of being the only chemist to discover an entire family of elements. Ramsay showed that the atmosphere contained a previously undiscovered gas, which he named argon. From air he also extracted and named krypton, neon, and xenon. He showed that the element previously believed to exist only in the sun, helium, was a member of the inert gas family. Ramsay received the 1904 Nobel Prize in chemistry for his chemical discoveries.

Chemical discovery continued throughout the 1900s. However, most scientists who made the advances did not wear the title chemist. Chemistry became intertwined with other areas of study, including physics, nuclear energy, and biology. American physicist Robert Millikan (1868–1953) made the first direct measurement of the charge on a single electron. Austrian-born Swedish physicist Lise Meitner (1878–1968) discovered that the uranium atom could divide into two smaller atoms with a tremendous release of energy. Danish physicist Niels Bohr (1885–1962) developed the modern model of the atom in which electrons have distinct energy levels. American physicist Arthur Holly Compton (1892–1962) used x-rays and the orderly nature of crystals to learn more about the properties of light. American physicists John Bardeen (1908–1991) and William Bradford Shockley (1910–1989) used the semiconducting properties of silicon to replace vacuum tubes with transistors. Bardeen went on to make advances in superconductivity.

American chemist Linus Carl Pauling (1901–1994) established the nature

Splitting the atom

of the chemical bond. English biochemist Dorothy Crowfoot Hodgkin (1910–1994) built the first models of complex organic compounds such as vitamins. English biochemist Frederick Sanger (1918–) showed the order of amino acids in protein molecules. He was the first to map a complete DNA molecule. English chemist Rosalind Elsie Franklin (1920–1958) made x-ray diffraction photographs that were crucial to understanding DNA. Her photography helped American biochemist James Dewey Watson (1928–) and English biochemist Francis Crick (1916–) decode the structure of DNA molecule.

What does it take to be a good chemist? Successful chemists know about their subject. They also have a broad education in other fields such as biology, geology, physics, mathematics, and computer science. Most chemists today work as a team. They see the usefulness of learning to speak and write effectively. The most important traits are a never-ending curiosity, motivation, and an enjoyment of the subject.

Can a person be a Christian and a chemist? Certainly. Notice that in the list of the ten greatest chemists of all time that five — Boyle, Faraday, Dalton, Pasteur, and Ramsay — can be described as Christians. They gave their lives to the service of God. Others, such as Robert Millikan and Arthur Holly Compton were outspoken Christians. They believed in the Bible as the guide to their lives. These great scientists show that a career in chemistry does not necessarily weaken a person's faith. All Christians, regardless of their professions, face temptations that might come between them and standing right with God. Robert Boyle strengthened his faith by daily Bible study and prayer. His example is one that would benefit all Christians.

Chemistry is an exciting field of study. Much still needs to be done. Students who enter the field have the opportunity to make important and beneficial advances.

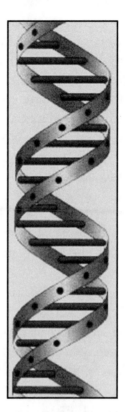

R E A C T I O N

1. Robert Boyle, John Dalton, and Henry Cavendish did much of their research without benefit of a large laboratory or trained assistants.

2. Louis Pasteur, William Ramsay, and others worked with assistants or partners.

3. Robert Millikan, Niels Bohr, and Lise Meitner were physicists; Dorothy Crowfoot Hodgkin and Frederick Sanger were biochemists.

Write the matching letter in the blank provided.

1. _____ helped found the Royal Society. He also defined an element.

2. _____ was an eccentric English chemist who discovered hydrogen.

3. _____ was a Frenchman who burned a diamond. He stated the law of conservation of matter.

4. _____ stated the atomic theory of matter.

5. _____ used electricity to free sodium and other elements from their ores.

6. _____ suggested the use of chemical symbols for elements.

7. _____ was Davy's assistant who discovered benzene.

8. _____ was a French chemist who became a medical researcher.

9. _____ made the first periodic table of the elements.

10. _____ discovered the family of inert gases.

    a. Jöns Jakob Berzelius
    b. Robert Boyle
    c. Henry Cavendish
    d. John Dalton
    e. Humphry Davy
    f. Michael Faraday
    g. Antoine Laurent Lavoisier
    h. Dmitri Ivanovich Mendeleev
    i. Louis Pasteur
    j. William Ramsay

Bibliography

Asimov, Isaac. *Asimov's Biographical Encyclopedia of Science and Technology*, second revised edition. (Garden City, NY: Doubleday & Company, Inc., 1982.)

Asimov, Isaac. *A Short History of Chemistry*. (Garden City, NY: Double & Company, Inc., 1965.)

Davis, Helen Miles; revisions by Glenn Seaborg. *The Chemical Elements*, 2nd Edition. (New York: Ballantine Books, Inc, 1959.)

Godman, Arthur. *Longman Illustrated Dictionary of Chemistry*. (Harlow, Essex, Britain: Longman Group Limited, 1982.)

Hall, A. Rupert and Marie Boas Hall. *A Brief History of Science*. (New York: Signet Science Library, 1964.)

Hart, Michael H. *The 100: A Ranking of the Most Influential Persons in History*. (Secaucus, NJ: Carol Publishing Group, 1993.)

McKenzie, A.E.E. *The Major Achievements of Science*. (New York: Simon and Schuster, 1960.)

Morris, Henry M. *Men of Science, Men of God*. (Green Forest, AR: Master Books, 1982.)

Poole, Lynn and Gray. *Scientists Who Changed the World*. (New York: Dodd, Mead & Co., 1962.)

Runes, Dagobert D., editor. *A Treasury of World Science*. (Paterson, NJ: Littlefield, Adams & Co., 1962.)

Seaborg, Glenn T. and Evans G. Valens. *Elements of the Universe*. (New York: E. P. Dutton & Company, Inc., 1958.)

Venetsky, S.I.; N.G. Kittell, translator. *Tales About Metals*. (Moscow: Mir Publishers, 1981.)

Internet Resources:

Biographies: <www.biography.com>

Nobel Prize winners: <www.nobel.se/prize/index.html>

Periodic Table Online: <www.shef.ac.uk/chemistry/web-elements/>

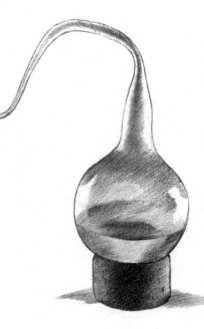

Answers to Chapter Questions

Chapter 1
1. meteorites
2. D
3. F
4. D
5. A
6. C
7. carbon
8. A
9. B
10. D
11. F
12. B

Chapter 2
1. copper
2. B
3. F
4. F
5. F
6. A
7. A
8. A
9. mercury
10. D
11. T
12. C
13. Mercury
14. D
15. A

Chapter 3
1. B
2. A
3. T
4. B
5. F
6. sulfuric
7. B
8. carbon
9. A
10. F
11. T
12. A
13. Dark
14. F
15. B
16. B
17. B

Chapter 4
1. A
2. B
3. D
4. A
5. A
6. T
7. D
8. D
9. A

10. A
11. B
12. T
13. A
14. B
15. H
    C
    N
    O
    Cl
16. H_2O
    CO_2
    HCl

Chapter 5
1. F
2. B
3. D
4. D
5. C
6. A
7. B
8. D
9. carbon
10. A
11. A
12. B
13. A
14. D

Chapter 6
1. B
2. B
3. D
4. B
5. B
6. D
7. T
8. A
9. C
10. D
11. F
12. F
13. A

Chapter 7
1. C
2. B
3. B
4. T
5. F
6. T
7. A
8. T
9. A
10. F
11. F
12. A
13. T

14. C
15. B

Chapter 8
1. B
2. B
3. T
4. F
5. F
6. C
7. atoms
8. A
9. B
10. A
11. C
12. A
13. B
14. B

Chapter 9
1. B
2. A
3. D
4. C
5. Sahara
6. F
7. C
8. B
9. B
10. B
11. Tyre
12. B

Chapter 10
1. B
2. T
3. C
4. A
5. A
6. B
7. B
8. B
9. F
10. B
11. B
12. B
13. A

Chapter 11
1. four
2. A
3. C
4. B
5. T
6. B
7. four
8. F
9. T
10. T
11. F

12. T
13. B
14. D
15. B
16. A
17. B
18. C

Chapter 12
1. B
2. A
3. carbon
4. F
5. F
6. A
7. B
8. D
9. C
10. F
11. F
12. D
13. A
14. F.
15. A

Chapter 13
1. nitrogen
2. B
3. T
4. F
5. nitrogen
6. D
7. A
8. B
9. B
10. T
11. C
12. F
13. D
14. A
15. T
16. F
17. T

Chapter 14
1. B
2. A
3. B
4. T
5. B
6. D
7. A
8. T
9. F
10. B
11. T
12. C
13. B

Chapter 15

1. F
2. T
3. A
4. A
5. F
6. A
7. F
8. T
9. T
10. A
11. C
12. T
13. F
14. A
15. T

Chapter 16
1. b
2. c
3. g
4. d
5. e
6. a
7. f
8. i
9. h
10. j

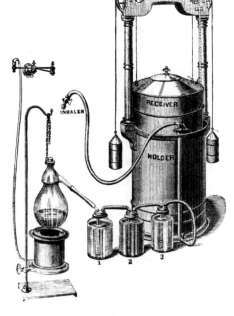

Index